T0330668

Leadership and Strategic Management
Decision-Making in Times of Change

Managers are facing unprecedented complexity, volatility, and ambiguity, quickly adapting their decision-making, leadership, vision, and strategies. Megatrends and forces of change have profound implications for business models, processes, and organizational structures, calling into question current paradigms and designing future change. Additionally, unprecedented disruptions, unforecastable in their nature, have increased the need for resilience and strategic flexibility.

The book aims at tackling the potential interrelations among environmental transformations, strategic decisions, and leadership to better understand the role of external and internal factors on the effectiveness of managers.

The book defines "change": its extent, nature, and characteristics. Then, it focuses on decision-making, the role of potential cognitive biases, and how the interaction with the perception of determined environmental events affects the way in which decision-makers decide to implement specific strategies. Finally, in the light of waves of strategic change, it reviews theories on leadership and transformation by looking at the role and traits of leaders.

Since environmental transformations have the potential to "disrupt" not only strategies but also decision-making processes and leadership, the book provides a review on the issue and propose an integrative framework which can be useful for both scholars and managers, especially in the fields of decision-making and strategy.

Paolo Boccardelli is a Full Professor of Management and Corporate Strategy at Libera Università Internazionale degli Studi Sociali University since 2004. He was Dean of the Luiss Business School from 2015 to May 2022. He is Director of the Research Center in Strategic Change "Franco Fontana" at Luiss University and Codirector of the Board Academy Program at Luiss Business School. His main areas of expertise are strategy and strategic planning, organization, and innovation.

Federica Brunetta is an Associate Professor of Management and Vice-Director of the Research Center in Strategic Change "Franco Fontana" at Luiss University. She is the Head of Executive Masters at Luiss Business School. Her main areas of expertise are strategic management, strategy in highly regulated industries, digital transformation, and strategic change.

Routledge Focus on Business and Management

The fields of business and management have grown exponentially as areas of research and education. This growth presents challenges for readers trying to keep up with the latest important insights. *Routledge Focus on Business and Management* presents small books on big topics and how they intersect with the world of business research.

Individually, each title in the series provides coverage of a key academic topic, while collectively, the series forms a comprehensive collection across the business disciplines.

Sustainable Governance in B Corps
Non-Financial Reporting for Sustainable Development
Patrizia Gazzola and Matteo Ferioli

Happiness and Wellbeing in Singapore
Beyond Economic Prosperity
Siok Kuan Tambyah, Tan Soo Jiuan and Yuen Wei Lun

Healthy Ageing after COVID-19
Research and Policy Perspectives from Asia
Edited by Wang-Kin Chiu and Vincent T.S. Law

Entrepreneurial Attributes
Accessing Your Inner Entrepreneur For Business and Beyond
Andrew Clarke

Leadership and Strategic Management
Decision-Making in Times of Change
Paolo Boccardelli and Federica Brunetta

For more information about this series, please visit: www.routledge.com/Routledge-Focus-on-Business-and-Management/book-series/FBM

Leadership and Strategic Management

Decision-Making in Times of Change

**Paolo Boccardelli and
Federica Brunetta**

Routledge
Taylor & Francis Group

NEW YORK AND LONDON

First published 2024
by Routledge
605 Third Avenue, New York, NY 10158

and by Routledge
4 Park Square, Milton Park, Abingdon, Oxon, OX14 4RN

Routledge is an imprint of the Taylor & Francis Group, an informa business

ISBN: 978-1-032-59800-0 (hbk)
ISBN: 978-1-032-60591-3 (pbk)
ISBN: 978-1-003-45980-4 (ebk)

DOI: 10.4324/9781003459804

Typeset in Times New Roman
by KnowledgeWorks Global Ltd.

Contents

About the Authors

Paolo Boccardelli

Full Professor of Strategy
Director of the Research Center for Strategic Change "Franco Fontana"
Luiss University, Department of Business and Management

Paolo Boccardelli is a Full Professor of Management and Corporate Strategy at Luiss University since 2004. He has been Dean of the Luiss Business School from 2015 to May 2022. He is Director of the Research Center in Strategic Change "Franco Fontana" and Codirector of the Board Academy Program at Luiss Business School. His main areas of expertise are strategy and strategic planning, organization, and innovations and operations management.

He is a Member of the Board of Directors, Chairman of the Related Parties Committee, and Member of the Control and Risk Committee of TIM Spa for the years 2021–2024. He is a Member of the Board of Directors and Chairman of the Related Parties Committee of Banco BPM. He has been a Member of the Board of Directors and President of the Remuneration Committee of UBI Banca.

He is a Member of the AACSB (Association to Advance Collegiate Schools of Business) Board of Directors, Member of the EQUIS Committee, and consultant for quality services and processes for schools that carry out EQUIS accreditation for the first time. He has been President of the Commissione di Vigilanza sulle Società di Calcio Professionistiche (Co.Vi.Soc.). He is a Member of the Board of Directors of Fondazione Nuovo Millennio and President of the Supervisory Board of Scuola Politica "Vivere nella comunità".

Federica Brunetta

Associate Professor of Management
Vice-Director of the Research Center for Strategic Change "Franco Fontana"
Luiss University, Department of Business and Management
Luiss Business School

Federica Brunetta is an Associate Professor of Management. She teaches General Management, Strategy, Economics of Strategy and Business

Transformation at Luiss Business School and at the Department of Business and Management.

She is Head of Executive Masters of Luiss Business School and Vice Director of the Research Centre in Strategic Change "Franco Fontana" of Luiss University.

Her research interests are focused on the study of strategies in highly regulated environments, digitalization and business transformation, and network analysis. Her works are published, among others, in *Organization Studies*, *Journal of Business Research*, *IEEE Transactions on Engineering Management*, and *Organizational Dynamics*.

She received her PhD from the Università Cattolica, and was a Visiting Scholar at the Ross School of Business, University of Michigan. She also received the Distinguished Paper Award from the Business Policy and Strategy Division of the Academy of Management.

Contributors

Chiara Acciarini is Post-Doc in Management Engineering at Sapienza University (Italy), she got a PhD in Management at Luiss University (Italy), where she is currently a Teaching Assistant for the Industrial Dynamics Master's Course. Her research is focused on strategic change, digital expertise of the board, and business model innovation.

Francesca Capo got a PhD in Management at Luiss Guido Carli University and has been a Visiting Scholar at ESSEC Business School (France), Catolica Business School (Portugal), and Ross School of Business (Michigan, US). Among her main research interests are category dynamics, institutional change, hybrid organizations, and social enterprises.

1 Leadership and Decision-Making in Times of Change

An Introduction

Federica Brunetta and Paolo Boccardelli

1.1 Introduction

The past few years, managers have had to deal with unprecedented complexity, volatility, and ambiguity, pushing them to quickly adapt decision-making, challenge leadership, and revise their vision and strategies. Megatrends and forces of change have deep implications for organizations, calling into question current processes and paradigms and setting the stage for future change. Additionally, we have experienced unprecedented disruptions, unable to be predicted by their very nature, increasing the need for resilience and strategic flexibility.

The book aims to take on the potential interrelations among environmental transformations (both in terms of forecastable trends and disruptive change), strategic decisions, and leadership to better understand the role of external and internal factors on the effectiveness of managers. It focuses on the research question: *How can managers and leaders better respond to environmental change?*

In the following paragraphs, we outline the content of the different chapters, with the aim of describing the major themes of this work.

1.2 The Facets of Change and Organizational Responses to It

The focus of the book is to understand how managers can navigate a dynamic environment characterized by change and transformation and adapt their decision-making and leadership accordingly. Therefore, because an initial and fundamental pillar of this work relates to defining change, the book starts by examining how change and transformation at the organizational level relate to socio-demographic, economic, technological, and environmental drivers and the macro level.

These transformations, defined as megatrends – when change depends on forces with global ramifications that are presently observable and expected to persist in the long term (European Commission, 2022) or disruptions if, on

DOI: 10.4324/9781003459804-1

the other hand, change is dependent on unforeseen occurrences that alter the trajectory of events unexpectedly (Cambridge University Press; Cambridge English Dictionary) – wield substantial potential to influence decision-making paradigms, business models, and organizational processes.

Chapter 2, authored with Acciarini and Capo, presents a review of the main megatrends and forces of change but also distinguishes the impact of disruptions and environmental jolts since these unforecastable occurrences within environments can lead to an altered landscape for organizations, for example redefining the boundaries of industries or markets and changing the level of available resources (Wan & Yiu, 2009).

Both observable megatrends and unexpected disruptions necessitate strategic foresight, planning, and resilience, meant as the ability to confront significant challenges and adapt accordingly while picking up on opportunities in spite of adversities (Linnenluecke, 2017; Williams & Shepherd, 2016). Therefore, Chapter 2 reviews the body of literature that has explored the diverse determinants of organizational resilience (e.g. Buliga et al., 2016; Iborra et al., 2020; Lengnick-Hall & Beck, 2005; Linnenluecke, 2017; Vogus & Sutcliffe, 2007) and also examines how strategic alliances and related collaborative decisions have emerged as a prospective solution for cultivating organizational resilience in response to transformation (e.g. Corbo et al., 2016; Dacin et al., 2007; Osiyevskyy et al., 2017; Pangarkar, 2003), going beyond the perspective of resilience as an outcome, but rather looking at it as a process (Bryce et al., 2022).

So, Chapter 2 lays the foundation for how to support flexibility, resilience, and dynamic capabilities as instrumental strategies to take on the complexity, volatility, and uncertainty inherent in these transformations.

1.3 Navigating Transformation: Decision-Making and Cognitive Biases in Dynamic Environments

While Chapter 2 focuses on defying change, Chapter 3 turns its attention to how managers should face that change and be able to make decisions in dynamic environments, especially in terms of how they are required not only to design, plan, and adopt new strategies but also to effectively implement them, and to seize opportunities in complex, uncertain situations (Sorrell et al., 2010). Success, indeed, relies on foresight – the ability to anticipate which strategic directions will produce positive results (Dranove et al., 2017). So, decision-making is crucial and relies on two essential skills, both contingent on individual capabilities: the ability to identify signals and the capability to analyze trends (Acciarini et al., 2020).

We specifically look at strategic decision-making (Elbanna, 2006) as it is crucial to the alignment of mission, core work, and goal achievement (Eisenhardt & Zbaracki, 1992). In particular, we focus on decision biases and institutions since they play a role in the decision-making process in dynamic environments with non-rational beliefs that impact the ability to make decisions grounded in data, evidence, and facts (Busenitz & Barney, 1997; Schwenk, 1986; Simon et al., 2000). These cognitive elements of decision-making relate to individuals that understand transformations based on their biases, perceptions, and values. In turn, distortions may be experienced, and outcomes may be impacted. We review Das and Teng's (1999) categorization of biases and their link to the different types of decision-making processes to understand the main implications for our work.

We also account for the relationships among decision-makers, organizations, and external institutions, and given the need to better understand the beliefs, values, and perceptions of decision-makers, we revise and investigate the significance of institutional logics meant as "socially constructed, historical patterns of material practices, assumptions, values, beliefs, and rules by which individuals produce and reproduce their material subsistence, organize time and space, and provide meaning to their social reality" (Thornton & Ocasio, 1999, p. 804).

Finally, we focus on trade-off between the use of intuition and rationality, as existing literature supports the idea that strategic decision-making incorporates elements of both processes (e.g. Calabretta et al., 2017; Dane & Pratt, 2007; Hunt et al., 1989; Miller & Ireland, 2005). More importantly, in dynamic environments, intuition (and the use of heuristics) appears as a crucial complement to rationality for strategic decision-making processes and to improve resilience (Calabretta et al., 2017; Dane & Pratt, 2007) since relying solely on rationality may prove ineffective due to the complexity and rapidity of change (Gigerenzer, 2008).

1.4   Leadership and Transformation

The final chapter, authored with Acciarini, concludes our work by focusing on transformation and the role of leaders in navigating and steering change because when they are confronted with transformation, uncertainty, and complexity, leaders must be ready to follow opportunities.

Vision is at the basis of strategic plans, and it is necessary to harmonize resources and capabilities, analyze scenarios, and harmonize goals and objectives. But vision is also dependent on leaders who need to possess those dynamic managerial capabilities necessary to manage and adapt to the transformations occurring in the external context, and reconfiguring the existing firm's resources, mission, and core work toward new strategies. This goes beyond merely adapting to these shifts; it involves leveraging them as catalysts for growth.

The chapter focuses on traits of leaders (Klemm, 2017) and, in particular, revises scholarly contributions related to personality traits (Judge & Long, 2012), leadership styles (Judge et al., 2009), skills and abilities (Antonakis, 2011; Judge et al., 2009; Zaccaro et al., 2018), emotional intelligence

(Antonakis, 2011; Tuncdogan et al., 2017; Zaccaro et al., 2018), or even "bright" and "dark" traits of leaders (Judge et al., 2009).

Finally, the chapter also focuses on transformative leadership (Caldwell et al., 2012), which has emerged in management literature as a new approach that focuses on empowering individuals and teams through shared vision and positive change.

In conclusion, the evolving business terrain demands leaders who embody adaptability and innovation, equipped with strategic vision, flexibility, and transformative leadership approaches. Managers can successfully navigate uncertainty and turbulence, especially leveraging on strategic decision-making, analysis, collaborations, and forecasting.

Organizations can prepare to navigate jolts and megatrends that may threaten their profitability and survival.

References

Acciarini, C., Brunetta, F., & Boccardelli, P. (2020). *Cognitive biases and decision-making strategies in times of change: A systematic literature review*. Management Decision.

Antonakis, J. (2011). Predictors of leadership: The usual suspects and the suspect traits. In A. Bryman, D. Collinson, K. Grint, B. Jackson, & M. Uhl-Bien (Eds), *Sage handbook of leadership* (pp. 269–285). Sage Publications.

Bryce, C., Ring, P., Ashby, S., & Wardman, J. K. (2020). Resilience in the face of uncertainty: Early lessons from the COVID-19 pandemic. *Journal of Risk Research*, *23*:7–8, 880–887. DOI: 10.1080/13669877.2020.1756379

Buliga, O., Scheiner, C. W., & Voigt, K.-I. (2016). Business model innovation and organizational resilience: Towards an integrated conceptual framework. *Journal of Business Economics*, *86*, 647–670. https://doi.org/10.1007/s11573-015-0796-y

Busenitz, L. W., & Barney, J. B. (1997). Differences between entrepreneurs and managers in large organizations: Biases and heuristics in strategic decision-making. *Journal of Business Venturing*, *12*(1), 9–30.

Calabretta, G., Gemser, G., & Wijnberg, N. M. (2017). The interplay between intuition and rationality in strategic decision making: A paradox perspective. *Organization Studies*, *38*(3–4), 365–401.

Caldwell, C., Dixon, R. D., Floyd, L. A., Chaudoin, J., Post, J., & Cheokas, G. (2012). Transformative leadership: Achieving unparalleled excellence. *Journal of Business Ethics*, *109*, 175–187.

Cambridge University Press. (2024). Disruption. In *Cambridge English Dictionary*. https://dictionary.cambridge.org/dictionary/english/disruption

Corbo, L., Corrado, R., & Ferriani, S. (2016). A new order of things: Network mechanisms of field evolution in the aftermath of an exogenous shock. *Organization Studies*, *37*, 323–348. https://doi.org/10.1177/0170840615613373

Dacin, M. T., Oliver, C., & Roy, J.-P. (2007). The legitimacy of strategic alliances: An institutional perspective. *Strategic Management Journal*, *28*, 169–187. https://doi.org/10.1002/smj.577

Dane, E., & Pratt, M. G. (2007). Exploring intuition and its role in managerial decision making. *Academy of Management Review, 32*, 33–54.

Das, T. K., & Teng, B. (1999). Cognitive biases and strategic decision processes: An integrative perspective. *Journal of Management Studies, 36*(6), 757–778.

Dranove, D., Besanko, D., Shanley, M., & Schaefer, S. (2017). *Economics of strategy.* John Wiley & Sons.

Eisenhardt, K. M., & Zbaracki, M. J. (1992). Strategic decision making. *Strategic Management Journal, 13*(S2), 17–37.

Elbanna, S. (2006). Strategic decision-making: Process perspectives. *International Journal of Management Reviews, 8*(1), 1–20.

European Commission. (2022). *The Megatrends Hub. Competence Centre on Foresight.* https://knowledge4policy.ec.europa.eu/foresight/tool/megatrends-hub_en

Gigerenzer, G. (2008). Why heuristics work. *Perspectives on Psychological Science, 3*, 20–29.

Hunt, R. G., Krzystofiak, F. J., Meindl, J. R., & Yousry, A. M. (1989). Cognitive style and decision making. *Organizational Behavior and Human Decision Processes, 44*(3), 436–453.

Iborra, M., Safón, V., & Dolz, C. (2020). What explains the resilience of SMEs? Ambidexterity capability and strategic consistency. *Long Range Planning, 53*(6), 101947.

Judge, T. A., & Long, D. M. (2012). Individual differences in leadership. *The Nature of Leadership, 2*, 179–217.

Judge, T. A., Piccolo, R. F., & Kosalka, T. (2009). The bright and dark sides of leader traits: A review and theoretical extension of the leader trait paradigm. *The Leadership Quarterly, 20*(6), 855–875.

Klemm, W. (2017). Leadership and creativity. In J., Marques, & S., Dhiman (Eds). *Leadership today: Practices for personal and professional performance* (pp. 263–278). Springer International Publishing Switzerland.

Lengnick-Hall, C. A., & Beck, T. E. (2005). Adaptive fit versus robust transformation: How organizations respond to environmental change. *Journal of Management, 31*, 738–757. https://doi.org/10.1177/0149206305279367

Linnenluecke, M. K. (2017). Resilience in business and management research: A review of influential publications and a research agenda. *International Journal of Management Reviews, 19*(1), 4–30. https://doi.org/10.1111/ijmr.12076

Miller, C. C., & Ireland, R. D. (2005). Intuition in strategic decision making: Friend or foe in the fast-paced 21st century? *Academy of Management Perspectives, 19*, 19–30.

Osiyevskyy, O., Tao, Q. T., Jiang, R. J., & Santoro, M. D. (2017). Opportunity is in the eye of beholder: Behavioral drivers of alliance portfolio adaptation to performance and environmental jolts. *The International Journal of Entrepreneurship and Innovation, 18*, 115–127. https://doi.org/10.1177/1465750317706623

Pangarkar, N. (2003). Determinants of Alliance duration in uncertain environments: The case of the biotechnology sector. *Long Range Planning, 36*, 269–284. https://doi.org/10.1016/S0024-6301(03)00041-4

Schwenk, C. H. (1986). Information, cognitive biases, and commitment to a course of action. *Academy of Management Review, 11*(2), 298–310.

Simon, M., Houghton, S. M., & Aquino, K. (2000). Cognitive biases, risk perception, and venture formation: How individuals decide to start companies. *Journal of Business Venturing, 15*(2), 113–134.

Sorrell, M., Komisar, R., & Mulcahy, A. (2010). How we do it: Three executives reflect on strategic decision making. *McKinsey Quarterly*, *2*, 46–57.

Thornton, P. H., & Ocasio, W. (1999). Institutional logics and the historical contingency of power in organizations: Executive succession in the higher education publishing industry, 1958–1990. *American Journal of Sociology*, *105*, 801–843.

Tuncdogan, A., Acar, O. A., & Stam, D. (2017). Individual differences as antecedents of leader behavior: Towards an understanding of multi-level outcomes. *The Leadership Quarterly*, *28*(1), 40–64.

Vogus, T. J., & Sutcliffe, K. M. (2007). Organizational resilience: Towards a theory and research agenda. *2007 IEEE International Conference on Systems, Man and Cybernetics*. Montreal, QC, Canada, 2007, pp. 3418–3422. DOI: 10.1109/ICSMC.2007.4414160

Wan, W. P., & Yiu, D. W. (2009). From crisis to opportunity: Environmental jolt, corporate acquisitions, and firm performance. *Strategic Management Journal*, *30*, 791–801. https://doi.org/10.1002/smj.744

Williams, T. A., & Shepherd, D. A. (2016). Building resilience or providing sustenance: Different paths of emergent ventures in the aftermath of the Haiti earthquake. *AMJ*, *59*, 2069–2102. https://doi.org/10.5465/amj.2015.0682

Zaccaro, S. J., Green, J. P., Dubrow, S., & Kolze, M. (2018). Leader individual differences, situational parameters, and leadership outcomes: A comprehensive review and integration. *The Leadership Quarterly*, *29*(1), 2–43.

2 The Facets of Change and Organizational Responses to It

Chiara Acciarini, Francesca Capo, Federica Brunetta, and Paolo Boccardelli

2.1 Introduction

Nowadays, organizations rise and are rooted on a shaky ground. The terrain organizations inhabit is becoming more and more precarious as they are constantly exposed to severe environmental disruptions and shifts, thus experiencing increasing uncertainty. So, they must be ready to anticipate and respond to shifts in the evolving landscape while also being able to proactively seek out new opportunities for growth and innovation.

Such challenges require organizations to be ready and able to navigate abrupt shifts and emergency situations, reacting quickly and adequately to external shocks and environmental jolts that may threaten their profitability and survival.

Therefore, organizations need a deep understanding of the trends, megatrends, and disruptions that are shaping the business environment; what's more, this time of unprecedented change requires a willingness to experiment, innovate, and take risks. However, despite the fact that most firms believe that innovation is a priority, only 20% of global businesses are already prepared and equipped to innovate (BCG, 2021).

This chapter focuses on change and transformation and how they are related to possible socio, demographic, economic, technological, and environmental drivers generating an impact on business models. We focus on megatrends, defined as fundamental forces of change, depictable by looking at trends with deep social, economic, and technological implications. While trends and megatrends are observable and can require planning, managers must also learn how to cope with potential disruptions that may act as catalysts or moderators of change. And learn how flexibility, resilience, and dynamic capabilities can be keys to face complexity, volatility, and uncertainty.

DOI: 10.4324/9781003459804-2

2.2   Times of Change? Trends, Megatrends, Disruptions, and Resilience

The business world is constantly evolving, and it is becoming even more complex, characterized by unprecedented change driven by a host of trends, megatrends, and disruptions that are transforming the way companies operate, compete, and innovate.

A trend can be defined as "a general development or change in a situation or in the way that people are behaving" (Cambridge University Press; Cambridge English Dictionary). More in general, we can refer to a gradual shift in consumer behavior, technology advancements, and market conditions that shape the business landscape over time. For instance, the rise of e-commerce and mobile technology has transformed the way consumers purchase, while the growth of social media has changed the way companies interact with their customers.

Megatrends are "Megatrends are defined as long-term driving forces that are observable now and will most likely have a global impact" (European Commission, 2022) and thus refer to more far-reaching shifts that have the potential to transform entire industries and economies. Megatrends are typically driven by larger societal changes, such as demographic shifts, climate change, and technological advancements. For example, artificial intelligence, robotics, and automation may disrupt the nature of work as we know it (Manyika et al., 2017). On the other hand, disruptions refer to "the action of completely changing the traditional way that an industry or market operates by using new methods or technology" (Cambridge University Press; Cambridge English Dictionary). They can be driven by technological advancements, regulatory changes, or even natural disasters. For example, the recent COVID-19 pandemic has caused widespread disruption across all sectors, forcing companies to reconfigure their business models and rapidly adapt to remote work and changing customer needs.

Extant research refers to the ability to face severe challenges and adjust by maintaining functions and "keep going" in spite of adversities (Williams & Shepherd, 2016) as resilience. Scholars in the management field have investigated the factors leading to resilience, exploring the variables that organizations may leverage to face crises, shocks, and disruptions and survive them. For example, O'Reilly & Tushman (2008) looked at the organizational ambidexterity and strategic consistency as potential tools for adapting to change. Other scholars have discussed the role of employee capacities to understand how organizations can improve their strengths (Luthans, 2002).

Researchers focused on the resource dependence theory (e.g. Burgelman & Grove, 1996; Kraatz & Zajac, 2001; Pfeffer, 1972; Pfeffer & Salancik, 2003) has consistently shown that organizations must be able to adapt their resources and competencies to these changing conditions to survive in the long term. Overall, companies are encouraged to develop a strategic mindset that emphasizes continuous learning, risk-taking, experimentation, and innovation to effectively manage complexity, volatility, and uncertainty.

Uncertainty, volatility, and complexity perfectly describe the main characteristics of new markets and represent crucial aspects that companies must consider building their own leadership and achieving a sustainable competitive advantage. Due to the rapid pace of technological progress, globalization, and geopolitical shifts, companies need to be able to shape new strategic choices to effectively manage and navigate these challenges.

Complexity refers to complicated situations producing high levels of interconnectedness, diversity, and unpredictability. In a complex business environment, firms interact with multiple stakeholders who have divergent interests; they also face rapid technological change, and they cope with specific regulatory frameworks. Therefore, to sense and respond quickly to new modifications, companies need to develop innovation, organizational flexibility, and adaptability, as well as the ability to collaborate with external partners to access resources and knowledge.

Volatility describes the degree of instability and turbulence of the business scenario. In a volatile environment, firms face sudden shocks, disruptions, and discontinuities that can threaten their survival. Moreover, based on an analysis of all the OECD countries, a 2015 report found that higher the volatility of a country's economy compared to its partners, the greater the propensity of its residents to invest in foreign assets (Fogli & Perri, 2015). The recent COVID-19 pandemic has disrupted the financial markets by generating high level of fluctuation in financial returns. To cope with volatility, companies need to take action on organizational resilience, which means the ability to absorb shocks, recover quickly, and learn from experience. Specifically, resilience is defined as the superior capacity of certain organizations, with respect to others, of promptly responding, recovering swiftly, or innovating business approaches during challenging circumstances (Linnenluecke, 2017). To increase the level of organizational resilience, companies can leverage the following:

- *Diversification of revenue lines* to amplify the ability to absorb demand volatility;
- *Launch of new product lines or new revenue models* to absorb risks and losses effectively;
- *Business system protection and defense* from the effects related to crises; and
- *More flexible cost structure.*

Uncertainty refers to the degree of ambiguity characterizing the business environment. In an uncertain environment, companies face multiple scenarios with varying degrees of risk and opportunity, and they must make strategic choices grounded on a limited set of information. To cope with uncertainty, companies need to develop the ability to anticipate, assess, and adapt to evolving trends and scenarios.

2.2.1   Megatrends and Forces of Change

The external environment where companies compete is influenced by several factors, including natural circumstances, technological advancements, cultural and social changes, and economic and political events. Below, we distinguish the different drivers of change within the external environment.

One of the main transformations characterizing our era is demographic evolution. Two hundred years ago, there were fewer than 1 billion living beings on our planet (Roser & Ortiz-Ospina, 2017); today, there are over 8 billion (Worldometer, 2023). The United Nations estimates that there is a 95% likelihood that the global population will grow to 8.4–8.7 billion by 2030, 9.4–10.2 by 2050, and 9.6–13.2 by 2100 (United Nations, 2017). The main drivers of this future demographic growth trend relate to birth rate, mortality rate, migration, and the current age distribution. Africa, the Middle East, and Southeast Asia are all seeing a population boom (Roser, 2017). Specifically, some nations, together, contribute to over 50% of the global population growth from 2017 to 2050, include (in simple alphabetical order) the Democratic Republic of the Congo, Egypt, Ethiopia, India, Indonesia, Nigeria, Pakistan, Uganda, United Republic of Tanzania, and the United States of America (United Nations, 2017). It should also be noted that almost 90% of the world's poor live in nations that are expected to see exponential population growth; moreover, if these areas were able to create jobs in line with the aforementioned growing trend, they could make the most of the potential to encourage development and reduce poverty in the years to come (Ahmed, 2015).

This demographic phenomenon represents only one of the most significant megatrends of the 21st century, capable of impacting businesses and, more generally speaking, transforming the world in the coming years. Another important issue is the aging of the population. An increase in population corresponds to a rise in the aging of the population: according to the World Economic Forum, the proportion of population over 60 years old may double by 2050 and triplicate by 2100 (United Nations, 2017). Life expectancy is increasing, and the cost of services is growing, along with the difficulty of designing effective welfare systems, which often do not meet expectations. Life expectancy is also increasing along with aging; a study conducted by several scientists from Imperial College London in collaboration with the World Health Organization and based on a sample of 35 industrialized countries, including Italy, shows an increase of at least 65% for women and 85% for men by 2030 (United Nations, 2017). Technological progress greatly contributes to this megatrend, and combined with the development of health devices, plays a pivotal role in enhancing the quality of life of individuals.

However, questions arise when it comes to people's ability to adapt to the surrounding context in which innovation and development represent the key drivers of change. For instance, in 2015, while 88.2% of Americans were reported to be Internet users, nearly 40% of individuals over 65 felt somewhat insecure in using computers, smartphones, or other electronic devices (11% of this category, moreover, claimed to be totally incapable of using them); among people aged between 18 and 29, less than 75% were certain they could use such devices, while the remaining part claimed total inability to do so (Anderson and Perrin, 2017). The speed at which technology evolves is impressive. Today, half of the world's population is connected, Internet users have grown by 1.9% over the past 12 months, and our minds can only imagine the potential for future advancement (We are Social, 2023).

The phenomenon of urbanization represents the future, as well: by 2050, at least 60% of the world's population will live in urban regions; in 2014, this percentage was already quite high and exceeded 50% (United Nations, 2014). Large urban centers are developing, the role of cities is growing, and their competition in terms of investments, companies, and jobs is increasing. The opportunities arising from these developing cities are manifold. An analysis conducted by Price Waterhouse Coopers highlights a series of advantages that residents can enjoy, including the achievement of economies of scale and the creation of value for people and companies, which are more involved socially. Innovation generates a virtuous circle that inspires productivity, the sharing of knowledge, and encouragement of talent. For example, developing cities can offer more efficient services, thus reducing costs and spurring further investment, and this benefits the entire community. Also, the relationship between economic growth and urbanization has been the subject of study over the years (Chen et al., 2014; Chenery & Taylor, 1968; Henderson, 2003): high urbanization rates often correspond to higher levels of GDP (Gross Domestic Product), which would explain the development of the economy. The elements that link the various urban centers are no longer just traditional; in an increasingly connected world, cities become integrated global network nodes that rely on digital infrastructure (Tranos et al., 2014). The progress of urbanization is astonishing: in the period between 2010 and 2025, the GDP of the top 600 cities in terms of contribution to GDP growth could increase by $30 trillion, equivalent to about 65% of global growth; moreover, the estimate becomes even more significant for emerging countries, which in the same period could represent almost half of the expected global GDP growth (Tranos et al., 2014). The evolution of urban centers is accompanied by a transformation of the consumer class, who should have a sufficient salary to buy essential goods, and will also be the class stimulating and driving the growth of demand for goods and services.

Constant innovation and rapid transformations that occur daily on a global scale are a consequence of human actions and can create numerous opportunities to be seized, as well as many challenges to face. However, not all individual behaviors generate benefits and advantages for the ecosystem. Take ongoing climate change, an impact produced by human actions to which governments and companies are responding extremely slowly. While the population is increasing, resources are becoming increasingly scarce: by 2025, 60% of the world's population could experience water shortages (WWF, 2023a); at the same time, the demand for water will grow at a rate of 2% per year, almost doubling by 2030 as compared to 2005 due to economic development (2030 Water Resources Group, 2009). The vicious circle is fueled by the production of CO_2 emissions, which, according to the WWF, cause global warming that will have devastating effects in the future for millions of people and even more so for those living in the most vulnerable areas of the world, where food production and living species, habitats, and ecosystems will be threatened and damaged (WWF, 2023b). Meanwhile, Italy reported the driest climate in the last 60 years in 2017 (Mastroianni, 2017); in 2022, The surface temperature exceeded the 20th-century average of 13.9°C by 0.86°C and was 1.06°C higher than the pre-industrial period (1880–1900). The warming of the Earth has led to the melting of glaciers, which by 2100 will flood entire cities, forcing about 200 million people to abandon their homes. Some of the countries most at risk include the Netherlands, Vietnam, Thailand, and Japan (Strauss, 2014). The Paris Agreement was created specifically to defend respect for and achieve environmental sustainability, with the objective of limiting the rise in the worldwide average temperature to less than 2°C. More recently, the Conference of Parties (COP) addressed climate change, engaged in negotiations, and implemented measures to tackle the issue. Some of the measures include, for example, leverage energy conversion devices – including, for example, engines and boilers – would increase their thermodynamic efficiency. In addition, energy savings could be connected to the reduction in demand for final energy services; this could be achieved through more efficient use of gasoline in the case of car travel, but also through reduced driving. In this sense, some progress has been made; for instance, the International Energy Agency observes that the global energy investment is increasing and that the global clean energy spending is ramping up (International Energy Agency, 2022). Moreover, the global sale of electric vehicles, which peaked in 2015, increased by more than 90% in 2022, contributing to significant savings in terms of energy consumption (International Energy Agency, 2023).

The middle classes are the driver of global growth, with this segment increasing from 899 million to 1.34 billion in the period between 2011 and 2019 (Pew Research Center, 2021), and with expected expansion over the coming years. For some years now, there has been a reverse trend as opposed to what happened following the financial crisis of 2007–2008, when, for example, Europe saw a decline in the middle class accompanied by an increase in inequality (International Labour Organisation, 2016). The middle-class trend takes hold rapidly and consistently in emerging economies, while it remains rather contained in countries characterized by slower development. For instance, by 2030, the middle-class population in Asia-Pacific could increase to 3.49 billion people (i.e., from 1.38 billion people in 2015) (Statista, 2023).

In contrast, the middle-class population in sub-Saharan Africa is projected to grow from 114 million in 2015 to 212 million by 2030. The middle class is growing and, along with it, the population's level of global consumption is increasing; in Brazil alone, total consumption reached more than 80% of GDP in 2021 (World Bank, 2021a). Another equally relevant phenomenon is represented by the Chinese market, where, despite contained GDP growth, it is possible to see a rapid increase in the level of consumption, which exceeded 54% of GDP in 2021 (World Bank, 2021b). Therefore, although the increasing trend has been observed globally, Asia appears to be the real center of development for the years to come.

The incredible speed at which technologies have developed and spread has allowed users, organizations, and companies around the world to connect with each other in real time, via a simple click, thus overcoming traditional physical barriers. With the expansion of digital technology, activities, and services have gradually become dematerialized, facilitating instantaneous exchange of information thanks to the integration between physical and digital channels. In fact, the technological factor plays a fundamental role in the creation of new distribution channels. The integration of markets, trade, and investments represent essential elements of the phenomenon of globalization, which generates new jobs, global economic growth, and greater competitiveness among companies, but it also produces greater inequality as well as unfair working and living conditions. The phenomenon of globalization, which has often been the subject of study, has generally been analyzed in relation to economic growth. In particular, a direct relationship can be seen between the economic globalization index and the development of the economies of emerging countries; for these latter, it would be advantageous that globalization may signify greater participation in international organizations, international trade, and foreign direct investment. According to the KOF Globalisation Index which measures the economic, social, and political dimensions of globalization (Dreher, 2006), the top-ranked countries worldwide are the Netherlands (90.91), Switzerland (90.45), Belgium (90.33), Sweden (89.44), and the United Kingdom (89.31).

Due to technological advancements and shifts in geopolitics, social, and environmental needs, a new phase of globalization has come about. This evolving trend requires concerted governance from multiple levels as well as higher engagement from stakeholders across societal and enterprise domains. More recently, with growing protectionism, after a year of war in Ukraine, and after the COVID-19 pandemic, globalization has declined for the first time since the Second World War, thus raising questions about whether it has reached its end (i.e., de-globalization) or if there is a resurgence. These new scenarios impose a strategy adaptation by decision-makers, who cannot ignore the specific needs of each country but rather must deal with a multitude of rules, economies, and technologies.

The incredible ability with which digital transformation is permeating entire sectors was effectively explained in 2015 by some authors from the Global Center for Digital Business Transformation, who compared the power of digital to a vortex, called the "digital vortex", which takes on the same characteristics of a rotary mechanism; in fact, everything converges towards the center, where business models, offerings, and value chains are digitized as much as possible. To understand how disruptive digital transformation it is enough to mention that, in view of digitalization, in the manufacturing sector, more than 35% of enterprises achieved above-average business value (Gartner, 2020). However, no sector is excluded: technology, media, retail, financial services, education, oil, and gas. More widespread Internet use allows processes, information, and people to be connected instantly, giving rise to a complex network called the Internet of Things (IoT). The advantages associated with digitization are numerous and significant, and organizations seem to have realized these opportunities: according to a study published in *MIT Sloan Management Review*, more than half of companies are adopting digital technologies to carry out their activities in innovative ways; however, almost 40% of them believe that there is a need to advance their digital strategy (Kane et al., 2017). Moreover, despite the fact that 37% of companies express concerns about automation putting jobs at risk (PwC, 2018), digital transformation has positive effects, including a decrease in global emissions of 15% (Börje & Rockström, 2019), in addition to the fact that, in 2021, mobile technologies and services generated 5% of GDP at global scale (World Bank, 2023). Europe, like the rest of the world, has already embarked upon a digitization process, with a boost of 250 billion euros from NextGenerationEU and with an estimate of 80% of the EU population equipped with basic digital skills by 2030 (European Commission, 2023).

The real challenge is to make business objectives consistent with actual strategic implementation. We already have examples of companies that have been able to seize the opportunities offered by digital transformation: Netflix has reinvented the world of digital entertainment, offering "on-demand" content that can satisfy a wide audience, while Amazon was the pioneer of digital books, allowing readers to buy reading materials at any time of the day, and even make it available instantly through the so-called Amazon Kindle, devices for reading e-books. What's more, the US e-commerce company has recently acquired the food giant Whole Foods, and, thanks to the extraordinary potential of digital technology, it is now possible to shop without going through the checkout, therefore without any waiting ("No lines. No checkout", as the company's slogan says). And, while in healthcare, there are already those who are adopting advanced technologies to produce organs for use in transplants, the hospitality industry sees the online portal Airbnb as a key player, allowing travelers from all over the world connect with those renting out accommodations. Even small companies, which have historically been less digitalized, saw bigger gains in digitalization after the COVID-19 pandemic (Jaumotte et al., 2023).

Overall, it is estimated that of the 60% of current occupations, at least 30% of activities can be automated (Manyika et al., 2017), with few tasks that can be fully automated. In the education sector, for example, most of the activities carried out outside of the classroom could be performed by new technologies, although human relationships and people skills still prevail in the teaching world. A research study conducted by the Bank of England reveals that sales & customer service, and manual labor are some of the professions with the highest risk of automation.

There is a lot of discussion now about replacing humans with both favorable and opposing opinions. According to analysts, digital strategies, such as what McDonald's implemented with the Experience of the Future (EOTF) technology, allowed the company to replace cashiers with digital kiosks in 2,500 restaurants in 2017, allowing customers to place orders independently. The role of machines is becoming increasingly prominent; however, human participation cannot be ignored, as it remains necessary to solve complex problems that require qualitative judgments. In the book "Artificial Intelligence: What Everybody Needs to Know", scientist and entrepreneur Jerry Kaplan addresses the topic of machines and the future of work, arguing that computers alone do not "think" but rather perform logical and deterministic actions, regardless of the complexity (Kaplan, 2016). In recent years, we have witnessed a real evolution in robots. They have gone from being industrial machines useful for the execution of specific programs to acquiring a greater degree of complexity and autonomy, allowing them to become service robots capable of understanding human actions and communicating with the surrounding environment, adapting to social norms. What is certain is that the ongoing digital transformation will radically change traditional approaches in the workplace. There will be a variety of possibilities for implementation and opportunities to be taken advantage of, with forms of involvement and smart solutions that coexist in a broader context where technology plays a fundamental role. The hope is that, in the future, complementary interaction between machines and human beings can be established, allowing for the intuitive thinking that technology lacks.

2.2.2 Disruptions and Environmental Jolts

Environmental opportunities and threats produce certain entrepreneurial actions that aim to create alignment between the firm and the external context (Hornsby et al., 2009; Liu et al., 2007). When environments surprise organizations, sudden and unprecedented events can happen, revealing a different nature. Some scholars referred to the concept of environmental jolts to explain the power that such events have in changing the levels of scenario predictability, which, in turn, affect strategy design and competitive advantage (Meyer et al., 1990). Furthermore, when environmental jolts occur, they can redefine the boundaries of an entire sector (Wan & Yiu, 2009). While Corbo et al. (2016) looked at the cataclysmic nature of upheavals like the terrorist attacks in the aftermath of September 11, 2001, Meyer et al. (1990) presented an unprecedented strike by physicians as the primary cause of a simultaneous voluntary hospital jolt. We follow the definition of (Wan & Yiu, 2009), who interpreted environmental jolts as a type of external context that considerably changes the level of resources available.

Typically, environmental jolts "can harm entrepreneurial firms" (Liu et al., 2007); in these cases, they are defined as "disruptive environmental jolts", leading to the most intense changes in the competitive environment (Tao et al., 2015). New opportunities for entrepreneurs and new organizational forms emerge (Meyer et al., 1990) in other circumstances. Extant research agrees that, in order to take on environmental jolts, organizations need to be resilient (Luthans, 2002; Sullivan-Taylor & Branicki, 2011) and able to quickly adjust to shocks undermining their profitability and survival.

2.3   Organizational Resilience as a Solution to Overcome Unexpected Events

Organizational resilience represents an important issue for strategic management research. In general, it has been studied in relation to the threatening nature of unexpected events. A unique conceptualization of organizational resilience has not existed until now. Typically, it is considered a "desirable characteristic" useful for taking on difficulties in dynamic environments (Buliga et al., 2016; Holling, 1973; Linnenluecke, 2017; Vogus & Sutcliffe, 2007). Especially according to some scholars (Holling, 1973), organizational resilience is the ability to tolerate changes and damages in turbulent environments. Therefore, organizations need to be resilient in order to avoid major consequences when unexpected events come about (Linnenluecke, 2017).

Extant research has explored the main determinants of improved organizational resilience when environmental jolts occur. For instance, for small and medium-sized enterprises (SMEs), Iborra et al. (2020) explored the role of strategic consistency and organizational ambidexterity in rendering these organizations more resilient. In addition, other scholars (Sullivan-Taylor & Branicki, 2011) have found a link between SMEs with limited resources and the need to become "more strategic and proactive" in managing external threats. The same authors suggested that, in order to be more resilient, these organizations need customized guidance on how to respond to unexpected events or regulations to support financial resources to deal with uncertainty. In the case of large firms, research has focused on specific preventative actions to unexpected events with the aim of understanding how these organizations can be prepared for disruptions (Linnenluecke, 2017; Weick & Sutcliffe, 2015).

Other strategies for taking on exogenous jolts and being more resilient (Lengnick-Hall & Beck, 2005) have to do with carrying out organizational routines, which, in turn, reduce complexity and uncertainty. In this sense, as suggested by Boisot and Child (1999), routines are considered a way to be aligned with the environment and to be particularly useful in enabling organizations to optimally manage resources and internal capabilities. Also, the study by Lengnick-Hall and Beck (2005) associated a certain HR system configuration with the ability to develop organizational resilience. Specifically, Implementing approaches such as promoting problem-solving capabilities, defining a clear purpose, possessing intellectual and social resources, and adopting iterative, reflective learning substantially boost an organization's adaptability to sudden changes, thereby strengthening resilience during challenging times.

2.4 The Role of Alliances and Collaborations in Fostering Organizational Resilience

Despite existing literature having discussed the variety of determinants of organizational resilience in times of environmental jolts, strategic alliances are considered as a potential solution for fostering organizational resilience and the ability to react to them. In fact, as discussed in the previous section, articulating and implementing collective responses rather than individual ones may be decisive in overcoming the negative consequences triggered by environmental jolts.

Strategic alliances are defined as cooperative relationships helping firms to share risk and protect resources (Eisenhardt & Schoonhoven, 1996). Strategic alliances "allow firms to pool resources in order to gain efficiencies in the use of existing resources" (Krishnan et al., 2016, p. 2536). Granovetter (1992) interpreted strategic alliances as opportunities to interact, while (Podolny, 1994) referred to the possibility to directly cooperate.

In the face of external changes, adjustments in terms of the strategic alliances portfolio represent a possible solution for organizations to remain flexible and to reduce their risk of exposure (Osiyevskyy et al., 2017). In addition, the same authors (Osiyevskyy et al., 2017) argued that modifications in size and governance diversity of the strategic alliances portfolio are "proactive strategies" enhancing the firm's competitive position in response to environmental jolts. Also, as discussed by Pangarkar (2003, p. 271) in relation to the biotechnology sector, in highly uncertain and rapidly evolving environments, the formation of alliances represents a "competitive necessity".

By examining the dynamics of interorganizational tie formation and dissolution, Corbo et al. (2016) scrutinized the role of interorganizational affiliations when exogenous shocks arise. In particular, they found that members of a network tend to respond to negative shocks by pursuing a hybrid network structure, thus coming together in the face of a significant threat. However, though research has focused on strategic alliances, in some cases, pointing out that alliances may be helpful for organizations facing shocks, it has not yet provided a clear explanation about how these strategies allow organizations to foster resilience, thus eventually being able to successfully navigate the negative consequences triggered by environmental jolts.

Indeed, strategic alliances lead organizations to deal with complexity in a cooperative way (Granovetter, 1992; Podolny, 1994). In particular, this strategy can be seen as a way to share risk among different parties and to find new opportunities when uncertain events arise (Marhold & Kang, 2017; Osiyevskyy et al., 2017). In general, previous research (e.g. Pangarkar, 2003) has discussed the role of strategic alliances in reducing the uncertainty that may characterize the external environment. While reducing uncertainty is certainly critical in the face of continuous turbulence, organizations need to learn what it takes to stand when a crisis hits.

Strategic alliances enable organizations to share resources and competencies (Das & Teng, 2000), providing them the possibility to build a solid pool of knowledge, financial resources, employees, and infrastructures to rely on in the face of challenges. Indeed, such resource slack enjoyed by organizations that cooperate through strategic alliances may come to be even more critical when outside resources come to be drastically depleted as in the case of crisis environmental jolts that trigger negative outcomes. This is because access to such pools of resources may provide organizations with the needed tools to face crisis, rendering them more resilient to jolts.

Also, literature has acknowledged that strategic alliances may be a flywheel in institutional terms, with organizations that – by forging alliances with other organizations – may increase their legitimacy and, consequently, their performance (Dacin et al., 2007). Showing conformity to social norms and expectations, and thus being legitimated, is key for every organization to get support from the needed stakeholders. While this is true in ordinary times, it may be especially the case in the face of environmental jolts, events that abruptly shift industry boundaries, and the priorities of actors within these markets. Indeed, when crises hit, stakeholders will have few means to sustain organizations, in need of accurately selecting a few partners and organizations to entrust and support. In these circumstances, it is clear that stakeholders will entrust and support organizations that are deemed more legitimate, with the consequence that these organizations, once adequately supported, will be more resilient and provided with the adequate tools to navigate the crisis.

In summary, in time of environmental jolts, strategic alliances provide organizations with a pool of resources and legitimacy able to foster their resilience.

Another important issue is the effect of institutional proximity in the relationship between strategic alliances and organizational resilience. Indeed, scholars define proximity as a valuable source of organizational resilience, able to affect the nature of relationships since resilient firms tend to look for other resilient firms (centralized effect) (e.g. Mithani, 2017). However, different types of proximity exist. Ahead of "spatial proximity", whose role in fostering organizational resilience has been investigated by scholars (Mithani et al., 2021), research has also acknowledged the existence of "institutional proximity" (Boschma, 2005). Specifically, "institutional proximity" indicates how close organizations are between each other in terms of both the informal institutions they incorporate (e.g. values, beliefs) and the formal institutions they abide (e.g. rules, laws) (Hong & Su, 2013). Ceteris paribus, two organizations that share the same value system (or, for example, the same language), are considered to be closer in institutional terms than organizations who do not. Some scholars agree that such proximity may ease the interaction between firms (Hong & Su, 2013) and reduce uncertainty and risk (Hong & Su, 2013; Zukin & DiMaggio, 1993). Others point to the detrimental effect such institutional closeness may have on the ability of organizations to generate innovative ideas and trigger novel opportunities: relying on similar value systems or beliefs may lock organizations into one or few logics, preventing them to grasp the innovative recombination potential that can be triggered when multiple logics are in place (Jay, 2013).

In this light, different but institutionally close organizations will experience less tension by sharing similar ideational elements, thus interacting more smoothly (Hong & Su, 2013). Strategic alliances provide the organizations involved with a greater pool of resources (tangible and intangible, such as legitimacy) to draw from. If organizations are institutionally close, the process of resource sharing will be less conflictual, triggering less tension and allowing the same organizations to smooth processes and decision-making; in this sense, they are able to prioritize what is needed to face the environmental jolt and to be more resilient.

Resilience is indeed a process, not an outcome (Bryce et al., 2022) that organizations follow to manage anticipation, response, or readjustment (Meyer, 1982) to the unexpected. Research has investigated these three arenas of resiliency (Bhamra et al., 2011) by accounting for, among other things, the severity of conditions (Sutcliffe & Vogus, 2003), decision-makers cognitive biases, and diverse perception of the environment (Acciarini et al., 2020; Shepherd et al., 2015). Nonetheless, although the presence of "weak signals" may help in foreseeing and, thus, in anticipating events, the response can become very complex.

Whenever jolts happen, resilience may ensure for organizations an effective functioning or even survival (Bryce et al., 2022; Weick & Sutcliffe, 2007). Organizations are required "to investigate, to learn, and to act without knowing in advance what one will be called to act upon" (Wildavsky, 1988, p. 77). In this light, it is actions such as innovating, being open, or working across boundaries (Bryce et al., 2022) that may support facing unexpected complex situations, along with the ability to deploy the right resources, which are more often found in a network of actors and rather than in a focal firm alone (e.g. Powell et al., 1996). Organizations are opting for cooperative efforts – via inter-organizational relationships – in order to reduce rather than develop internal capabilities necessary for success (Oliver, 1990). Strategic alliances are vehicles used by organizations to respond to complex, dynamic environments. Benefits of sharing resources have widely been discussed (e.g. Doz et al., 1989; Perks & Easton, 2000), and so the chance to learn new or enhance existing capabilities (Kogut, 1988).

2.5 Conclusions

Businesses are not new to environmental jolts. Nonetheless, thus far, they have mostly maintained continuity even in face of health crises (Bryce et al., 2022), financial crises (Hausman & Johnston, 2014), conflicts, terrorism, and environmental disasters; and for the most part, they have recovered quickly, leveraging on resilience. Major jolts, such as the 2008 financial crisis, had a dual impact (Hausman & Johnston, 2014). On the one hand, companies anticipated a decline in demand, leading them to formulate strategies focused on survival through cost reduction. On the other hand, the decrease and uncertainty in demand led to a reduction in stock or access to internal resources. Nonetheless, the COVID-19 pandemic showed peculiar differences (Chesbrough, 2020); it has changed the way organizations have responded, driven by the need for a fast response, sought at the macro level, incentivizing collective and individual initiatives, aimed at finding responses both to the virus and to the quest for an adaptation of the economic activities of organizations around the globe.

Within this context, emphasis on time and speed of solutions, rather than costs, has determined a much bigger emphasis on collaboration (Chesbrough, 2020), providing opportunities to all actors in the system and to the system itself. Users have also played a role, as they themselves benefited from the solutions, and have become a non-conventional source of collaboration (Chesbrough, 2020; Von Hippel, 2006).

A second major point is to better understand what would make such collaborations more suitable and effective. Network scholars have devoted much attention to understanding the effects of networking on resource sharing or knowledge transfer (e.g. Gupta & Polonsky, 2014; Powell et al., 1996, 2005) and the motivation of partners to exchange such resources and knowledge.

In summary, through strategic decision-making, analysis, collaborations, and forecasting, managers can successfully navigate uncertainty and turbulence, especially in times of change. As pointed out by Chesbrough (2020), openness and collaboration, with diverse actors in the ecosystem, were essential elements in responding to the pandemic, and to crises as well, but it is also a good practice to employ these things on a daily basis. Organizations can prepare to navigate jolts and megatrends that may threaten their profitability and survival.

References

2030 Water Resources Group (2009). *Charting Our Water Future, Economic Frameworks to Inform Decision-Making,* MGI (McKinsey Global Institute)

Acciarini, C., Brunetta, F., & Boccardelli, P. (2020). *Cognitive biases and decision-making strategies in times of change: A systematic literature review.* Management Decision.

Ahmed, S. A. (2015). *How are global demographics changing?.* World Economic Forum. https://www.weforum.org/agenda/2015/10/how-are-global-demographics-changing/

Anderson, M., & Perrin, A. (2017). *Tech adoption climbs among older adults, barriers to adoption and attitudes towards technology.* Pew Research Center.

BCG (2021). *Overcoming the Innovation Readiness Gap.* Boston Consulting Group. Available online at: https://web-assets.bcg.com/eb/93/cfbea005442482b0adc64b9f499f/bcg-most-innovative-companies-2021-apr-2021-r.pdf

Bhamra, R., Dani, S., & Burnard, K. (2011). Resilience: The concept, a literature review and future directions. *International Journal of Production Research, 49*(18), 5375–5393.

Boisot, M., & Child, J. (1999). Organizations as adaptive systems in complex environments: The case of China. *Organization Science, 10,* 237–252. https://doi.org/10.1287/orsc.10.3.237

Börje, E., & Rockström, J. (2019). *Digital technology can cut global emissions by 15%. Here's how.* World Economic Forum.

Boschma, R. (2005). Role of Proximity in Interaction and Performance: Conceptual and Empirical Challenges. Regional Studies: The Journal of the Regional Studies Association, 39(1), 41–45.

Bryce, C., Ring, P., Ashby, S., & Wardman, J. K. (2020). Resilience in the face of uncertainty: Early lessons from the COVID-19 pandemic. *Journal of Risk Research, 23*(7–8), 880–887. https://doi.org/10.1080/13669877.2020.1756379

Buliga, O., Scheiner, C. W., & Voigt, K.-I. (2016). Business model innovation and organizational resilience: Towards an integrated conceptual framework. *Journal of Business Economics, 86,* 647–670. https://doi.org/10.1007/s11573-015-0796-y

Burgelman, R. A., & Grove, A. S. (1996). Strategic dissonance. *California Management Review, 38*(2), 8–28.

Cambridge University Press. Disruption. In *Cambridge English Dictionary.* Accessed 2024. Available online at: https://dictionary.cambridge.org/dictionary/english/disruption

Cambridge University Press. Trend. In *Cambridge English Dictionary.* Accessed 2024. Available online at: https://dictionary.cambridge.org/dictionary/english/trend

Chen, M., Zhang, H., Liu, W., & Zhang, W. (2014). *The global pattern of urbanization and economic growth: Evidence from the last three decades.* US National Library of Medicine, National Institutes of Health.

Chenery, H. B., & Taylor, L. (1968). Development patterns: Among countries and over time. *The Review of Economics and Statistics, 50*(4), 391–416.

Chesbrough, H. (2020). To recover faster from Covid-19, open up: Managerial implications from an open innovation perspective. *Industrial Marketing Management, 88,* 410–413.

Corbo, L., Corrado, R., & Ferriani, S. (2016). A new order of things: Network mechanisms of field evolution in the aftermath of an exogenous shock. *Organization Studies, 37,* 323–348. https://doi.org/10.1177/0170840615613373

Dacin, M. T., Oliver, C., & Roy, J.-P. (2007). The legitimacy of strategic alliances: An institutional perspective. *Strategic Management Journal, 28*, 169–187. https://doi.org/10.1002/smj.577

Das, T. K., & Teng, B.-S. (2000). A resource-based theory of strategic alliances. *Journal of Management, 26*, 31–61. https://doi.org/10.1177/014920630002600105

Doz, Y., Hamel, G., & Prahalad, C. (1989). Collaborate with your competitors and win. *Harvard Business Review, 67*, 133–139.

Dreher, A. (2006). Does globalization affect growth? Evidence from a new index of globalization, *Applied Economics, 38*(10), 1091–1110.

Eisenhardt, K. M., & Schoonhoven, C. B. (1996). Resource-based view of strategic alliance formation: Strategic and social effects in entrepreneurial firms. *Organization Science, 7*, 136–150. https://doi.org/10.1287/orsc.7.2.136

European Commission (2022) The Megatrends Hub. Competence Centre on Foresight. Retrieved November 2023, from https://knowledge4policy.ec.europa.eu/foresight/tool/megatrends-hub_en

European Commission (2023). A Europe Fit for the Digital Age. Empowering People with a New Generation of Technologies. Retrieved November 2023 from https://commission.europa.eu/strategy-and-policy/priorities-2019-2024/europe-fit-digital-age_en

Fogli, A., & Perri, F. (2015). Macroeconomic Volatility and External Imbalances. *National Bureau of Economic Research Working Paper Series, 20872, 10.3386/w20872.* https://www.nber.org/system/files/working_papers/w20872/w20872.pdf

Gartner (2020). Digital Transformation in Manufacturing. Available online at: https://www.gartner.com/en/industries/manufacturing-digital-transformation.

Granovetter, M. (1992). Economic institutions as social constructions: A framework for analysis. *Acta Sociologica, 35*, 3–11. https://doi.org/10.1177/000169939203500101

Gupta, S., & Polonsky, M. (2014). Inter-firm learning and knowledge-sharing in multinational networks: An outsourced organization's perspective. *Journal of Business Research, 67*(4), 615–622.

Hausman, A., & Johnston, W. J. (2014). The role of innovation in driving the economy: Lessons from the global financial crisis. *Journal of Business Research, 67*(1), 2720–2726.

Henderson, V. (2003). The urbanization process and economic growth: The so-what question. *Journal of Economic Growth, 8*, 47–71.

Holling, C. S. (1973). Resilience and stability of ecological systems. *Annual Review of Ecology and Systematics, 4*, 1–23. https://doi.org/10.1146/annurev.es.04.110173.000245

Hong, W., & Su, Y.-S. (2013). The effect of institutional proximity in non-local university–industry collaborations: An analysis based on Chinese patent data. *Research Policy, 42*, 454–464. https://doi.org/10.1016/j.respol.2012.05.012

Hornsby, J. S., Kuratko, D. F., Shepherd, D. A., & Bott, J. P. (2009). Managers' corporate entrepreneurial actions: Examining perception and position. *Journal of Business Venturing, 24*, 236–247. https://doi.org/10.1016/j.jbusvent.2008.03.002

Iborra, M., Safón, V., & Dolz, C. (2020). What explains the resilience of SMEs? Ambidexterity capability and strategic consistency. *Long Range Planning, 53*(6), 101947.

International Energy Agency (2022). *World Energy Investment. Retrieved on October 2023 from https://www.iea.org/reports/world-energy-investment-2022*

International Energy Agency (2023). *Global EV Outlook 2023. Analysis. Retrieved on October 2023 from https://www.iea.org/reports/global-ev-outlook-2023*

International Labour Organisation (2016). Executive summary: *Long Term Trends in the World of Work: Effects on Inequalities and Middle-Income Groups*. Retrieved on October 2023 from: https://www.ilo.org/brussels/press/press-releases/WCMS_455739/lang--en/index.htm

Jay, J. (2013). Navigating paradox as a mechanism of change and innovation in hybrid organizations. *Academy of Management Journal, 56*, 137–159. https://doi.org/10.5465/amj.2010.0772

Kane, G. C., Palmer, D., Phillips, A. N., Kiron, D., & Buckley, N. (2017). Achieving digital maturity adapting your company to a changing world. *MIT Sloan Management Review, 56*(1), 137–159.

Kaplan, J. (2016). *Artificial intelligence: What everyone needs to know*. Oxford University Press.

Kraatz, M. S., & Zajac, E. J. (2001). How organizational resources affect strategic change and performance in turbulent environments: Theory and evidence. *Organization Science, 12*(5), 632–657.

Krishnan, R., Geyskens, I., & Steenkamp, J.-B. E. M. (2016). The effectiveness of contractual and trust-based governance in strategic alliances under behavioral and environmental uncertainty: Effectiveness of contracts and trust under uncertainty. *Strategic Management Journal, 37*, 2521–2542. https://doi.org/10.1002/smj.2469

Lengnick-Hall, C. A., & Beck, T. E. (2005). Adaptive fit versus robust transformation: How organizations respond to environmental change. *Journal of Management, 31*, 738–757. https://doi.org/10.1177/0149206305279367

Linnenluecke, M. K. (2017). Resilience in business and management research: A review of influential publications and a research agenda. *International Journal of Management Reviews, 19*(1), 4–30. https://doi.org/10.1111/ijmr.12076

Liu, T.-H., Hung, S.-C., & Chu, Y.-Y. (2007). Environmental jolts, entrepreneurial actions and value creation: A case study of trend micro. *Technological Forecasting and Social Change, 74*, 1432–1445. https://doi.org/10.1016/j.techfore.2006.05.010

Luthans, F. (2002). The need for and meaning of positive organizational behavior. *Journal of Organization Behavior, 23*, 695–706. https://doi.org/10.1002/job.165

Manyika, J., Chui, M., Miremadi, M., Bughin, J., George, K., Willmott, P., & Dewhurst, M. (2017). *A future that works: Automation, employment, and productivity*. McKinsey Global Institute.

Marhold, K., & Kang, J. (2017). The effects of internal technological diversity and external uncertainty on technological alliance portfolio diversity. *Industry and Innovation, 24*, 122–142. https://doi.org/10.1080/13662716.2016.1216396

Mastroianni, F. (2017). *2017: È stato l'ottobre più secco degli ultimi 60 anni. Il meteo e il clima, Il Sole 24 Ore*. Retrieved on September 2023 from https://www.infodata.ilsole24ore.com/2017/12/21/lottobre-piu-secco-degli-ultimi-60-anni-sara-linverno-verra/

Meyer, A. D. (1982). Adapting to environmental jolts. *Administrative Science Quarterly, 27*(4), 515–537.

Meyer, A. D., Brooks, G. R., & Goes, J. B. (1990). Environmental jolts and industry revolutions: Organizational responses to discontinuous change. *Strategic Management Journal, 11*, 93–110.

Mithani, M. A. (2017). Liability of foreignness, natural disasters, and corporate philanthropy. *Journal of International Business Studies*, *48*, 941–963. https://doi.org/10.1057/s41267-017-0104-x

Mithani, M. A., Gopalakrishnan, S., & Santoro, M. D. (2021). Does exposure to a traumatic event make organizations resilient?. *Long range planning*, *54*(3), 102031.

Oliver, C. (1990). Determinants of interorganizational relationships: Integration and future directions. *Academy of Management Review*, *15*(2), 241–265.

O'Reilly, C. A., & Tushman, M. L. (2008). Ambidexterity as a dynamic capability: Resolving the innovator's dilemma. *Research in Organizational Behavior*, *28*, 185–206. https://doi.org/10.1016/j.riob.2008.06.002

Osiyevskyy, O., Tao, Q. T., Jiang, R. J., & Santoro, M. D. (2017). Opportunity is in the eye of beholder: Behavioral drivers of alliance portfolio adaptation to performance and environmental jolts. *The International Journal of Entrepreneurship and Innovation*, *18*, 115–127. https://doi.org/10.1177/1465750317706623

Pangarkar, N. (2003). Determinants of alliance duration in uncertain environments: The case of the biotechnology sector. *Long Range Planning*, *36*, 269–284. https://doi.org/10.1016/S0024-6301(03)00041-4

Perks, H., & Easton, G. (2000). Strategic alliances: Partner as customer. *Industrial Marketing Management*, *29*(4), 327–338.

Pew Research Center (2021). *The pandemic stalls growth in the global middle class, pushes poverty up sharply*. Retrieved on November 2023 from https://www.pewresearch.org/global/wp-content/uploads/sites/2/2021/03/PG_2021.03.18_Global-Middle-Class_FINAL.pdf

Pfeffer, J. (1972). Merger as a response to organizational interdependence. *Administrative Science Quarterly*, *17*, 382–394.

Pfeffer, J., & Salancik, G. R. (2003). *The external control of organizations: A resource dependence perspective*. Stanford University Press.

Podolny, J. M. (1994). Market uncertainty and the social character of economic exchange. *Administrative Science Quarterly*, *39*, 458. https://doi.org/10.2307/2393299

Powell, W. W., Koput, K. W., & Smith-Doerr, L. (1996). Interorganizational collaboration and the locus of innovation: Networks of learning in biotechnology. *Administrative Science Quarterly*, *41*(1), 116–145.

Powell, W. W., White, D. R., Koput, K. W., & Owen-Smith, J. (2005). Network dynamics and field evolution: The growth of interorganizational collaboration in the life sciences. *American Journal of Sociology*, *110*(4), 1132–1205.

PwC (2018). *Workforce of the Future. The Competing Forces Shaping 2030*. Retrieved online October 2023 at https://www.pwc.com/gx/en/services/workforce/publications/workforce-of-the-future.html

Roser, M. (2017). *Future Population Growth*. Published online at OurWorldInData.org. Available online at: https://ourworldindata.org/future-population-growth

Roser, M., & Ortiz-Ospina, E. (2017). *World Population Growth*. Published online at OurWorldInData.org. Available online at: https://ourworldindata.org/world-population-growth/

Shepherd, D. A., Williams, T. A., & Patzelt, H. (2015). Thinking about entrepreneurial decision making: Review and research agenda. *Journal of Management*, *41*(1), 11–46.

Statista (2023). *Forecast of the Global Middle Class Population from 2015 to 2030, by Region.* Retrieved in November 2023 from https://www.statista.com/statistics/255591/forecast-on-the-worldwide-middle-class-population-by-region/

Strauss, B. (2014). *New Analysis Shows Global Exposure to Sea Level Rise.* Research Report by Climate Central. Retrieved in November 2023 from https://www.climate central.org/news/new-analysis-global-exposure-to-sea-level-rise-flooding-18066

Sullivan-Taylor, B., & Branicki, L. (2011). Creating resilient SMEs: Why one size might not fit all. *International Journal of Production Research, 49*, 5565–5579.

Sutcliffe, K. M., & Vogus, T. J. (2003). Organizing for resilience. *Positive Organizational Scholarship: Foundations of a New Discipline, 94*, 110.

Tao, Q. T., Jiang, R. J., & Santoro, M. D. (2015). Expand or retrench? Alliance portfolio adaptation to environmental jolts. *IJBE, 7*, 79. https://doi.org/10.1504/IJBE.2015.066004   https://www.climatecentral.org/news/new-analysis-global-exposure-to-sea-level-rise-flooding-18066

Tranos, E., Kourtit, K., & Nijkamp, P. (2014). Digital urban network connectivity: Global and Chinese internet patterns. *Papers in Regional Science, 93*(2), 409–428.

United Nations (2014). *Department of Economic and Social Affairs.* Available online at: http://esa.un.org/unpd/wup/Highlights/WUP2014-Highlights.pdf

United Nations (2017). World population 2017. Department of Economic and Social Affairs World Population prospects. https://www.un.org/development/desa/pd/sites/www.un.org.development.desa.pd/files/files/documents/2020/Jan/un_2017_world_population_prospects-2017_revision_databooklet.pdf

Vogus, T. J., & Sutcliffe, K. M. (2007). Organizational resilience: Towards a theory and research agenda. *2007 IEEE International Conference on Systems, Man and Cybernetics.* Montreal, QC, Canada, 2007, pp. 3418–3422, doi: 10.1109/ICSMC.2007.4414160

Von Hippel, E. (2006). *Democratizing innovation.* The MIT Press.

Wan, W. P., & Yiu, D. W. (2009). From crisis to opportunity: Environmental jolt, corporate acquisitions, and firm performance. *Strategic Management Journal, 30*, 791–801. https://doi.org/10.1002/smj.744

We are Social (2023). Digital 2024 Report. Available at: https://wearesocial.com

Weick, K. E., & Sutcliffe, K. M. (2007). Managing the unexpected: What business can learn from high reliability organizations. Managing the Unexpected: Resilient Performance in an Age of Uncertainty. 2nd Edition. San Francisco: Jossey-Bass.

Weick, K. E., & Sutcliffe, K. M. (2015). *Managing the unexpected: Sustained performance in a complex world* (3rd ed.). Wiley.

Wildavsky, A. B. (1988). *Searching for safety* (Vol. 10). Routledge.

Williams, T. A., & Shepherd, D. A. (2016). Building resilience or providing sustenance: Different paths of emergent ventures in the aftermath of the Haiti earthquake. *AMJ, 59*, 2069–2102. https://doi.org/10.5465/amj.2015.0682

World Bank (2021a). *Final Consumption Expenditure (% of GDP) – Brazil.* https://data.worldbank.org/indicator/NE.CON.TOTL.ZS?locations=BR

World Bank (2021b). *Final Consumption Expenditure (% of GDP) – China.* https://data.worldbank.org/indicator/NE.CON.TOTL.CD?locations=CN

World Bank (2023). *Digital Development.* Retrieved online September 2023. https://www.worldbank.org/en/topic/digitaldevelopment

Worldometer. (2023). *World Population Index*. https://www.worldometers.info/

WWF (2023a). *Water Scarcity Trends*. Retrieved online October 2023. https://www.worldwildlife.org/threats/water-scarcity

WWF (2023b). *Climate Change*. Retrieved online October 2023. https://www.worldwildlife.org/threats/effects-of-climate-change

Zukin, S., & DiMaggio, P. (Eds.). (1993). *Structures of capital: The social organization of the economy (reprinted.)*. Cambridge University Press.

3 Navigating Transformation
Decision-Making and Cognitive Biases in Dynamic Environments

Federica Brunetta and Paolo Boccardelli

3.1 Introduction

Transformations in times of change require managers not only to design, plan, and adopt new strategies but also to effectively implement them and to seize opportunities in complex, uncertain situations (Sorrell et al., 2010). This chapter focuses on strategic decision-making: a non-routinary, long-term planning process that aligns with organizational objectives and goals and leads to the definition of a firm's strategy (Eisenhardt, 1999; Elbanna, 2006). More specifically, strategic decisions relate to planning, steering strategic direction, and allocating resources and competencies to support goal achievement (Eisenhardt & Zbaracki, 1992), therefore, being able to quickly define high-quality strategic choices is crucial for a successful strategy, enabling organizations to achieve and protect their advantage on the competitive landscape (Baum & Wally, 2003; Dean & Sharfman, 1996, 1993).

In general, managers operate in a landscape characterized by complexity and uncertainty, with potential outcomes that are unpredictable and conditions, such as consumer preferences, technological advancements, or decisions made by diverse stakeholders that are not clearly defined (Dranove et al., 2017). This is to say that environmental uncertainty is a critical factor to strategic design and for decisions about resource planning and allocation (Bukszar, 2009; Hogarth & Makridakis, 1981; Stubbart, 1989).

Of course, employing tools like economic modeling may support managers in navigating intricate complexities by breaking them up into more manageable challenges. However, the application of models only provides insights about realities that are nuanced by constraints imposed by both external and internal factors (Dranove et al., 2017).

The ability to navigate the implementation of strategic decisions, change, and the reconfiguration of internal structures is crucial to a firm's success. Nonetheless, managers do not work via hindsight, and timing is key. Within this context, strategic decision-making hinges on two critical abilities, both dependent on personal capabilities. Firstly, the capacity to spot signals and, secondly, the ability to interpret trends (Acciarini et al., 2020; Caldwell et al., 2012).

DOI: 10.4324/9781003459804-3

In order to be able to seize opportunities, managers – and organizations – must identify change at the embryonic stage, spotting "weak signals" that are described by Ansoff (1980, p. 12) as "warnings (external or internal), events and developments that are still too incomplete to permit an accurate estimation of their impact and/or to determine their full-fledged responses". More recently, Reeves et al. (2021, p. 96) have referred to potential, impactful change as being signaled by mere anomalies, so "weak signals that are, in some way, surprising but not entirely clear in scope or import". Finally, weak signals have also been referred as trends (Von Groddeck and Schwarz, 2013), and as such, hard to identify in terms of ramifications and temporal span.

Spotting signals is crucial to avoiding "strategic surprises" because success, contrary to a mere retrospective assessment, hinges upon foresight – the capacity to envisage which strategic pathways will yield favorable outcomes (Dranove et al., 2017). Indeed, once a trend is established, the opportunities become clearer to competitors, and making the most of the advantages becomes more complex. At the same time, many anomalies remain as such and do not lead to meaningful trends, making the desire to navigate change even harder for decision-makers (Reeves et al., 2021). Failure to detect "weak signals" (Ansoff, 1980) may lead to an incomplete interpretation of events, making planning and implementing specific strategies very complex.

Since the effective implementation of new strategies by managers requires decision-makers to detect signals and recognize trends, this chapter explores whether particular decision biases and institutions play a role in the decision-making process, especially in dynamic environments, with biases seen as non-rational beliefs influencing rational decision-making based on facts and evidence (Busenitz & Barney, 1997; Schwenk, 1986; Simon et al., 2000). The chapter also goes more in-depth about how extent decision-makers are able to leverage the trade-off between intuitive and rational decision-making while also taking into account the role of new technologies and data analytics.

3.2   Cognitive Elements and Strategic Decisions

Chapter 2 of this book outlined change and transformations, with a specific emphasis on those situations catalyzed by megatrends – great forces like demographic shifts, urbanization, digitization, and workforce evolution, with implications for decision-making frameworks, business models, and internal processes.

Nonetheless, identifying and navigating these transformations goes beyond collecting data and making observations; managers gather and assess all relevant information, employing both rational and intuitive approaches (Calabretta et al., 2017). So, it necessitates cognitive conceptualization and is contingent upon the cognitive systems of decision-makers. Cognition is defined as the different processes involving the transformation, reduction, elaboration, storage, retrieval, and utilization of sensory inputs (Neisser, 1967), encompassing both information collection and processing activities. Seidl (2004, p. 157) affirmed that any cognitive system actively engages with its environment, but the nature and manner of this engagement are predominantly determined by the cognitive system itself rather than the external environment.

Cognition is pivotal in understanding transformation and consequent decision-making processes. So, any related implication impacts significantly on managerial understanding of the environment and its potential scenarios and subsequent strategic decision-making. Building upon Simon's (1957) description of a decision as a complex social process typically spanning a significant amount of time, strategic decisions typically require an analysis of external and internal elements in order to properly allocate resources and competencies (Chandler, 1962; Shrivastava & Grant, 1985), reach specific outcomes, and steer the organizational trajectory and structure (Eisenhardt & Zbaracki, 1992).

Simon (1947) highlighted managerial limitations in achieving purely rational decisions due to computational constraints, information scarcity, and inherent biological limits, which constitute the concept of bounded rationality. This boundedness manifests in limitations having to do with perception, memorization, the representation of alternatives, access to information, and the cognitive architecture's inability to evaluate all potential alternatives (Simon, 1947). Thus, information collection and processing are intrinsic to enhanced environmental interpretation. Factors influencing this interpretation process include management beliefs on analyzability, environmental attributes, the inquirer's experience, the nature of the sought-after answer, and the methodologies employed in information acquisition, filtration, processing, and analysis (Daft & Weick, 1984).

The cognitive aspects of decision-makers, such as judgment and problem representation, may introduce distortions, as individuals read change relying on personal perceptions, values, and biases (Acciarini et al., 2020). Managerial heterogeneity in perceptions regarding the physical and social environment is well-documented in literature (Acciarini et al., 2020; Cristofaro, 2016, 2017, 2020; Hristov et al., 2022), which has found it to be influenced by relational and political factors (Eisenhardt & Zbaracki, 1992; Elbanna, 2006; Whittington, 2001), the cognitive traits of decision-makers (Amason, 1996; Keh et al., 2002; Miller et al., 1998; Simon et al., 2000; Wiersema & Bantel, 1992), perception of time horizon and timespan (Das & Teng, 1999), diversity (Knight et al., 1999; Olson et al., 2007), affective states (Cristofaro, 2016, 2017, 2020; Liu & Maitlis, 2014; Maitlis, 2005), personality styles (Cristofaro, 2016), and demographic characteristics (Forbes, 2005; Wiersema & Bantel, 1992).

In general, "systematic cognitive dispositions or inclinations in human thinking and reasoning that often do not comply with the tenets of logic, probability reasoning, and plausibility" (Korteling & Toet, 2020) are referred to as *cognitive biases*. Biases encompass both *heuristics* and *traps* (Cristofaro & Giannetti, 2021). Heuristics are basic "rules of thumb" or "cognitive shortcuts" that speed up and simplify complex decisions, but despite being useful and also necessary in certain situations, they may introduce biases in the decision process that can have effects – positive or negative – in decision-making (Artinger et al., 2015; Cristofaro, 2017; Cristofaro & Giannetti, 2021; Kahneman et al., 1982). On the other hand, traps are cognitive errors that always negatively impact decisions (Cristofaro & Giannetti, 2021; Hammond et al., 1998).

If we assume that ambiguity and uncertainty are embedded into strategic decisions and that biases are inherently intuitive and subconscious and are found at the basis of judgments (Das & Teng, 1999), strategic decision-makers are likely to experience cognitive biases (James & Barnes, 1984; Schwenk, 1986), and strategic decisions often relate to the application of biases and heuristics (Busenitz & Barney, 1997). This relationship will impact both decision-making processes (Das & Teng, 1999) and behavioral outcomes (Korteling & Toet, 2020).

As suggested by Das and Teng (1999), biases are pivotal and consistently factor into strategic decision-making processes and strategic planning through various facets. Cognitive biases can be categorized in different ways but mainly pertain to anchoring on prior hypotheses and a narrow focus, constrained exposure to alternatives, disregard for the probability of certain outcomes, and the illusion of control over situations (Das & Teng, 1999; March & Shapira, 1987).

Specifically, following Das and Teng's (1999) categorization, the first bias relates to *Having Prior Hypotheses and Focusing on Limited Targets,* implying that managers often rely on their pre-existing hypotheses or beliefs during the decision-making processes. These prior perceptions might cause them to overlook contradictory information that challenges their established views (Schwenk, 1984), and additionally, they may put a greater emphasis on select goals instead of broader objectives (March & Shapira, 1987). A second bias has to do with *Exposure to Limited Alternatives*, as managers may often limit themselves to considering a few restricted strategic avenues or multiple courses of action in order to achieve specific goals (March & Shapira, 1987) because they use sequential evaluation and intuition (March & Simon, 1958). This tendency results in a constrained view of available choices. The third type of bias described by Das and Teng (1999) has to do with *Insensitivity to Outcome Probabilities*. In other words, decision-makers typically show a lack of trust and understanding and don't rely on estimates (and how valid they are) regarding outcome probabilities. The result is that they may end up prioritizing the value of potential outcomes over the actual probabilities associated with them (Shapira, 1995). The fourth and final type of bias has to do with the *Illusion of Manageability* and actually takes on two forms: first, decision-makers tend to perceive higher success probabilities and develop an illusion of control over outcomes, forming overly optimistic estimates and disregarding inherent risks. Second, decision-makers may hold the belief that consequences stemming from their choices are controllable, developing the idea of "post-decisional control".

Of course, the effect of a cognitive bias may depend on the type of decision-making process applied (Das & Teng, 1999). Following Das and Teng (1999), we refer to five main types of decision-making processes. First, *rational* decision-making (Allison, 1971; March & Simon, 1958), whereby managers tend to follow a logical and systematic process to evaluate alternatives and to maximize outcomes, so the biases related to prior hypotheses and illusion of manageability may have a stronger impact on the process. In *avoidance* decision-making modes (Cyert & March, 1963; Das & Teng, 1999), individuals or groups seek to evade making choices or confront challenges, with the first three forms of biases playing a major role. In *logical incrementalist* decision-making modes (Quinn, 1980), gradual, incremental adjustments to decisions are made, so the illusion of manageability seems to be a dominant factor. A fourth decision-making style is the *political mode* (Baldridge, 1971), which accounts for power dynamics and politics, with decisions based on negotiations, bargaining, and the pursuit of individual or group interests within the organization. In this scenario, the limitations of targets and prior hypotheses will likely impact strategic choices. Finally, the decision-making process known as *garbage can* mode (Cohen et al., 1972) sees it as a chaotic process where problems, solutions, and decision-makers intersect randomly, and choices may depend more on situational factors than deliberate planning. Again, the availability of alternatives, as well as insensitivity to outcome probabilities, are biases that may influence such decision processes more than others.

3.2.1 The Role of Institutional Frameworks and Logics

Since organizations often react to external pressures by conforming to and satisfying the demands set by established and stable institutional components (DiMaggio & Powell, 1991), another important factor that impacts decision-making is the role of institutions (De Cian et al., 2020; Teixeira et al., 2017). Extant literature (DiMaggio, 1988; DiMaggio & Powell, 1983; North, 1991; Oliver, 1990, 1991, 1997; Peng, 2002; Peng et al., 2009) acknowledges the substantial impact of institutional frameworks on a firm's behavior, pointing out that strategic decisions are influenced by pluralistic, formal, and informal constraints (Meyer & Rowan, 1977).

It is therefore important to account for the dynamic relationships among individuals, organizations, and external institutions. Here, we focus on the significance of institutional logics – broader belief, value, and assumption systems that shape the cognition and actions of actors, determining what is meaningful and legitimate (Batista et al., 2015; Friedland & Alford, 1991; Lounsbury, 2007; Teixeira et al., 2017; Thornton & Ocasio, 2008) in light of the historical, procedural, and social aspects of decisions.

Logics influence the development of normative behaviors and suggest sets of potential actions, thus defining templates – both cognitive and practical – that decision-makers may follow (Kubra Canhilal et al., 2016; Pache & Santos, 2010, 2013). Nonetheless, organizations are likely to incorporate multiple logics, and each may embed different (even conflicting) values and principles that determine priorities in goals and strategies (Thornton & Ocasio, 1999, 2008). In turn, these potentially conflicting logics may impact the cognition of managers and, therefore, their decision-making (Besharov & Smith, 2014; Cobb et al., 2016; Smith et al., 2013; Yan et al., 2018) and even create "organizing tensions" (Smith et al., 2013) with a subsequent impact on the outcomes of their decisions.

Institutional logics provide, at the macro level, broader patterns of beliefs and socially shared constructs. At the individual, micro level, people pay attention to logics during social interactions but situational cues will affect how accessible, available, and noticeable these logics are (Ocasio, 1999). This focus triggers mechanisms impacting not only decision-making but also sensemaking, and the definition of identities and related practices within organizations. Consequently, the identity and the organizational practices strengthen and refocus an individual's attention while also influencing the evolution of macro-level institutional logics (Glaser et al., 2016). This model (see Thornton et al., 2012, p. 85 for a description of the Cross-Level Model of Institutional Logics) also proposes that logics models an individual's behavior through the definition of schemas, identities, and goals.

Thus, literature agrees that institutional logics shape actors' cognition and thus impact decision-making (Thornton & Ocasio, 1999, 2008). Usually, an organization's positioning toward institutional logics is reflected in mission, strategy, structure, identity, and core work (Besharov & Smith, 2014; Greenwood & Suddaby, 2006; Thornton et al., 2005). Nonetheless, the impact of logic multiplicity may vary: some organizations are deeply influenced by various logics, shaping their core mission and strategy, while others are predominantly driven by single logics with any additional logic having a marginal influence (Besharov & Smith, 2014). In this light, Besharov and Smith (2014) propose two critical dimensions – centrality and compatibility – as measures for this diversity, with centrality showing the extent (low or high) of relevance within organizational features, and compatibility related to the level (low or high) of alignment of multiple logics with actions and choices.

The combination of these dimensions describes four types of organizations: contested, estranged, aligned, and dominant. Contested organizations are characterized by low compatibility and high centrality. In these types of organizations, multiple logics produce significant influence, resulting in potential conflicts. Decision-makers within the organization may, therefore, struggle with divergent goals, values, and practices that cause ambiguity in setting practices and priorities and create competing expectations among members. Estranged organizations, on the other hand, display low compatibility and low centrality. Despite the presence of a primary logic, these organizations experience subsidiary logics that may conflict with the dominant one. While conflicts are moderate rather than extensive, there's consistent tension arising from the coexistence of different logics. Aligned organizations show high compatibility and high centrality. In such settings, multiple logics strongly influence the organization, but they also align consistently with the organization's core mission and strategy. While there may be potential for conflict due to the coexistence of various logics, this alignment minimizes conflicts. However, there might be some ambiguity as individuals don't receive clear signals related to the prevailing logic. Finally, dominant organizations exhibit high compatibility but low centrality. In such organizations, there is a single dominant logic that significantly shapes core organizational features and is reflected across mission, strategy, identity, and practices. Any additional subsidiary logic tends to align with the primary logic, so limited or no conflicts arise.

In this review, we have highlighted how institutional logics may play a pivotal role in decision-making processes (Besharov & Smith, 2014; Cobb et al., 2016; Durand et al., 2013; Glaser et al., 2016; Greenwood & Suddaby, 2006; Thornton & Ocasio, 1999; Thornton et al., 2005, 2012). Nonetheless, the extent to which these logics are embraced or contested is reflected in an organization's core (mission, strategy, structure, and identity) and resonates within the decision made (Besharov & Smith, 2014). Undoubtedly, multiple logics within organizational frameworks shape decision-making, but they also serve as valuable resources that an organization may deploy to drive strategic choices (Durand et al., 2013), underlining the importance of institutional frameworks in guiding organizational choices.

3.3   The Trade-Off between Intuition and Rationality in Decision-Making

Existing studies describe decision-making as a rational or normative process involving sequential, methodical collection and analysis of available information, enabling decision-makers to select the most rational and logical alternative (Cabantous & Gond, 2011; Elbanna, 2006; Hitt & Tyler, 1991; Papadakis & Barwise, 1997). Nonetheless, as we have observed above, this process is "boundedly rational" (Eisenhardt & Zbaracki, 1992) or "quasi-rational" (Shrivastava & Grant, 1985) due to the inherent cognitive biases in information processing for decision-makers.

So, while scholars have often emphasized the dominance of rational, analytical procedures in influencing choices (De Martino et al., 2006), emotional or intuitive responses also have a significant influence on human decision-making. Literature supports the idea that strategic decision-making embeds both components of rational analysis and intuition (Allinson et al., 2000; Andersen, 2000; Calabretta et al., 2017; Hunt et al., 1989; Khatri & Alvin, 2000; Miller & Ireland, 2005; Plessner et al., 2011; Sadler-Smith & Shefy, 2004), in which the latter – unlike rationality – is defined as the rapid, subconscious identification of trends, structures, and patterns supporting analyses and assessments (Calabretta et al., 2017; Dane & Pratt, 2007).

This holds true in dynamic business environments, in which relying solely on analytical and rational decision-making processes may fail due to sudden changes, transformations, and challenges. Actually, in these settings, intuition seems necessary for strategic decision-making processes (Dane & Pratt, 2007; Dean & Sharfman, 1993; Hough & Ogilvie, 2005) along with the use of heuristics to make quick yet accurate decisions (Gigerenzer, 2008) to improve the firm's adaptability and resilience. Of course, intuition may be twofold: so-called *intuition-as-expertise* is the result of a learning process that encompasses both explicit and implicit knowledge derived from one's past experiences, practices, and feedback, while *intuition-as-feeling* involves relying on gut feelings to inform decision-making (Sadler-Smith & Shefy, 2004).

Therefore, extant literature supports the idea that an interplay between intuition and rationality is effective, as it can enhance an organization's capability to use the search space to explore and analyze data and gather details while, at the same time, gain a holistic perspective leveraging on experiences (Hodgkinson et al., 2009; Khatri & Alvin, 2000). Intuition is meant to mobilize lesser resources and require shorter times and limited effort (Gigerenzer, 2008; Miller & Ireland, 2005), so it may complement rationality and vice-versa (Calabretta et al., 2017). On the other hand, intuition does not often appear to be highly valued, particularly in managerial settings as intuition is often disregarded for a lack of transparency and decision-making accountability and is therefore not considered significant or even trustworthy (Gigerenzer, 2008). So this may lead to cognitive tensions (Calabretta et al., 2017; Dameron & Torset, 2014), with the risk of having decision-makers either rely on intuition or rationality rather than an integration of both, while the ability to balance them in decision-making is seen as more effective (Butler, 2002; Calabretta et al., 2017; Hodgkinson et al., 2009; Woiceshyn, 2009).

In dynamic environments, these tensions can be exacerbated (Fredrickson & Mitchell, 2018; Vassilis et al., 1998) because relying solely on comprehensive and perhaps lengthy, rational processes in strategic decision-making may hinder organizational performance (Fredrickson & Mitchell, 2018). Combining this with intuition-based decision-making would allow for quicker decisions, which are fundamental in dynamic environments

(Khatri & Ng, 2000). Of course, such balance is not easy and may depend on additional factors, such as the nature of the situation, the hierarchical position of the decision-makers (Vassilis et al., 1998), or their cognitive style, which may impact their perceived cause-effect logic of using intuition or rationality (Calabretta et al., 2017).

Nevertheless, today, major technological changes and the availability of tools like big data analytics and artificial intelligence have the potential to challenge traditional paradigms for decision-making, as well as moderate tensions in the trade-off between intuition and rationality (Gupta & George, 2016; Janssen et al., 2017; Merendino et al., 2018; Vidgen et al., 2017; Wang et al., 2016). Decisions can now be taken faster and more accurately (Pauleen & Wang, 2017). Indeed, the introduction of such technologies has disrupted the way people work at many levels, and this includes a shift in decision-making, both in terms of the knowledge available (Janssen et al., 2017) and potential authority. This is because it has changed the way senior management is tackling change, inspiring top and mid-level managers to shape their competencies accordingly (Merendino et al., 2018). The availability of big data, the speed of analysis, and the possibility of relying on artificial intelligence has, indeed, impacted the time needed for rational decision-making, optimizing operations and information collection, analysis, and interpretation (Gupta & George, 2016; Pauleen & Wang, 2017), and enabling strategic steering as strategies are rooted in organizational data with potentially higher success rates (Intezari & Gressel, 2017).

3.4   Conclusions

This chapter has focused on strategic decision-making and elements that may impact a manager's ability to make decisions that align with organizational goals and lead to a successful strategy.

Firstly, we looked at the role of potential cognitive biases and how a manager perceives the environment and decides to implement specific strategies. Since change and dynamism in the environment may potentially "disrupt" decision-making processes and strategies, an effective implementation of new, or adapted, strategies by managers requires managers to be able to identify signals and recognize trends.

Particular decision biases play a role in the decision-making process in dynamic environments and in different institutional frameworks, thus, a second point addressed in the chapter was the impact of diverse institutional logics at play.

Finally, decision-makers must be able to leverage the trade-off between intuitive and rational decision-making while taking into account the role of analytics, big data, AI, and new technologies. Needless to say, harnessing the potential of such technologies depends on investments in digital capabilities, the capability to embrace a data-driven approach, and the cognitive and digital competencies of decision-makers, which are critical for improving decision-making by predicting patterns (Bharadwaj et al., 2013; Janssen et al., 2017; Merendino et al., 2018).

References

Acciarini, C., Brunetta, F., & Boccardelli, P. (2020). Cognitive biases and decision-making strategies in times of change: A systematic literature review. *Management Decision, 59*(3), 638–652.

Allinson, C. W., Chell, E., & Hayes, J. (2000). Intuition and entrepreneurial behaviour. *European Journal of Work and Organizational Psychology, 9*, 31–43.

Allison, G. T. (1971). *Essence of decision. Explaining the Cuban missile crisis.* HarperCollins College Publishers.

Amason, A. C. (1996). Distinguishing the effects of functional and dysfunctional conflict on strategic decision making: Resolving a paradox for top management teams. *Academy of Management Journal, 39*(1), 123–148.

Andersen, J. A. (2000). Intuition in managers: Are intuitive managers more effective?. *Journal of Managerial Psychology, 15*, 46–63.

Ansoff, H. I. (1980). Strategic issue management. *Strategic Management Journal, 1*(2), 131–148.

Artinger, F., Petersen, M., Gigerenzer, G., & Weibler, J. (2015). Heuristics as adaptive decision strategies in management. *Journal of Organizational Behavior, 36*(S1), S33–S52.

Baldridge, J. (1971). *Power and conflict in the university: Research in the sociology of complex organizations.* John Wiley.

Batista, M. D. G., Clegg, S., Pina, Cunha, M., Giustiniano, L., & Rego, A. (2015). Improvising prescription. Evidence from the emergency room. *British Journal of Management, 27*(2), 406–425.

Baum, J. R., & Wally, S. (2003). Strategic decision speed and firm performance. *Strategic Management Journal, 24*, 1107–1129.

Besharov, M. L., & Smith, W. K. (2014). Multiple institutional logics in organizations: Explaining their varied nature and implications. *Academy of Management Review, 39*, 364–381.

Bharadwaj, A., El Sawy, O. A., Pavlou, P. A., & Venkatraman, N. V. (2013). Digital business strategy: Toward a next generation of insights. *MIS Quarterly, 37*(2), 471–482.

Bukszar, E. (2009). Strategic bias: The impact of cognitive biases on strategy. *Canadian Journal of Administrative Sciences, 16*, 105–117.

Busenitz, L. W., & Barney, J. B. (1997). Differences between entrepreneurs and managers in large organizations: Biases and heuristics in strategic decision-making. *Journal of Business Venturing, 12*(1), 9–30.

Butler, R. (2002). *Decision making* (A. Sorge, Ed.). Thomson Learning.

Cabantous, L., & Gond, J. P. (2011). Rational decision making as performative praxis: Explaining Rationality's Éternel Retour. *Organization Science, 22*(3), 573–586.

Calabretta, G., Gemser, G., & Wijnberg, N. M. (2017). The interplay between intuition and rationality in strategic decision making: A paradox perspective. *Organization Studies, 38*(3–4), 365–401.

Caldwell, C., Dixon, R. D., Floyd, L. A., Chaudoin, J., Post, J., & Cheokas, G. (2012). Transformative leadership: Achieving unparalleled excellence. *Journal of Business Ethics, 109*, 175–187.

Chandler, A. D. (1962). *Strategy and structure: Chapters in the history of American industrial enterprises* (Vol. 14). MIT Press.

Cobb, J. A., Wry, T., & Zhao, E. Y. (2016). Funding financial inclusion: Institutional logics and the contextual contingency of funding for microfinance organizations. *Academy of Management Journal, 59*, 2103–2131.

Cohen, M. D., March, J. G., & Olsen, J. P. (1972). A garbage can model of organizational choice. *Administrative Science Quarterly, 17*(1), 1–25.

Cristofaro, M. (2016). Cognitive styles in dynamic decision making: A laboratory experiment. *International Journal of Management and Decision Making, 15*(1), 53–82.

Cristofaro, M. (2017). Reducing biases of decision-making processes in complex organizations. *Management Research Review, 40*(3), 270–291.

Cristofaro, M. (2020). "I feel and think, therefore I am": An Affect-Cognitive Theory of management decisions. *European Management Journal, 38*(2), 344–355.

Cristofaro, M., & Giannetti, F. (2021). Heuristics in entrepreneurial decisions: A review, an ecological rationality model, and a research agenda. *Scandinavian Journal of Management, 37*(3), 101170.

Cyert, R. M., & March, J. G. (1963). *A behavioral theory of the firm, University of Illinois at Urbana-Champaign's Academy for entrepreneurial leadership historical research reference in entrepreneurship*. Prentice Hall.

Daft, R. L., & Weick, K. (1984). Toward a model of organizations as interpretation systems. *Academy of Management Review, 9*, 284–296.

Dameron, S., & Torset, C. (2014). The discursive construction of strategists' subjectivities: Towards a paradox lens on strategy. *Journal of Management Studies, 51*, 291–319.

Dane, E., & Pratt, M. G. (2007). Exploring intuition and its role in managerial decision making. *Academy of Management Review, 32*(1), 33–54.

Das, T. K., & Teng, B. (1999). Cognitive biases and strategic decision processes: An integrative perspective. *Journal of Management Studies, 36*(6), 757–778.

De Cian, E., Dasgupta, S., Hof, A. F., van Sluisveld, M. A., Köhler, J., Pfluger, B., & van Vuuren, D. P. (2020). Actors, decision-making, and institutions in quantitative system modelling. *Technological Forecasting and Social Change, 151*, 119480.

De Martino, B., Kumaran, D., Seymour, B., & Dolan, R. J. (2006). Frames, biases, and rational decision-making in the human brain. *Science, 313*(5787), 684–687.

Dean, J. W., & Sharfman, M. P. (1993). The relationship between procedural rationality and political behavior in strategic decision making. *Decision Sciences, 24*(6), 1069–1083.

Dean, J. W. Jr, & Sharfman, M. P. (1996). Does decision process matter? A study of strategic decision-making effectiveness. *Academy of Management Journal, 39*(2), 368–392.

DiMaggio, P. J. (1988). Interest and agency in institutional theory. In L. Zucker (Ed.), *Institutional patterns and organizations* (pp. 3–22). Ballinger.

DiMaggio, P. J., & Powell, W. W. (1983). The iron cage revisited: Institutional isomorphism and collective rationality in organizational fields. *American Sociological Review, 48*(2), 147–160.

DiMaggio, P. J., & Powell, W. W. (1991). Introduction. In *The new institutionalism in organizational analysis* (pp. 1–38). University of Chicago Press.

Dranove, D., Besanko, D., Shanley, M., & Schaefer, S. (2017). *Economics of strategy.* John Wiley & Sons.

Durand, R., Szostak, B., Jourdan, J., & Thornton, P. H. (2013). Institutional logics as strategic resources. In M. Lounsbury, & E. Boxenbaum (Eds.), *Institutional logics in action: Vol. Part A* (pp. 165–201). Emerald Group Publishing Limited.

Eisenhardt, K. M., & Zbaracki, M. J. (1992). Strategic decision making. *Strategic Management Journal, 13*(S2), 17–37.

Eisenhardt, K. M. (1999). Strategy as strategic decision making. *MIT Sloan Management Review, 40*(3), 65.

Elbanna, S. (2006). Strategic decision-making: Process perspectives. *International Journal of Management Reviews, 8*(1), 1–20.

Forbes, D. P. (2005). Are some entrepreneurs more overconfident than others? *Journal of Business Venturing, 20*(5), 623–640.

Fredrickson, J. W., & Mitchell, T. R. (2018). Strategic decision processes: Comprehensiveness and performance in an industry with an unstable environment. *Academy of Management Journal, 27*, 399–423.

Friedland, R., & Alford, R. R. (1991). Bringing society back in: Symbols, practice and institutional contradictions. In W. W. Powell, & P. J. DiMaggio (Eds.), *The new institutionalism in organizational analysis* (pp. 232–263). University of Chicago Press.

Gigerenzer, G. (2008). Why heuristics work. *Perspectives on Psychological Science, 3*, 20–29.

Glaser, V. L., Fast, N. J., Harmon, D. J., & Green, S. E. Jr. (2016). Institutional frame switching: How institutional logics shape individual action. In J., Gehman, M. Lounsbury, & R. Greenwood (Eds.), *How institutions matter!* (pp. 35–69). Emerald Group Publishing Limited.

Greenwood, R., & Suddaby, R. (2006). Institutional entrepreneurship in mature fields: The big five accounting firms. *Academy of Management Journal, 49*(1), 27–48.

Gupta, M., & George, J. F. (2016). Toward the development of a big data analytics capability. *Information & Management, 53*(8), 1049–1064.

Hammond, S. H., Keeney, R. L., & Raiffa, H. (1998). The hidden traps in decision. *Harvard Business Review, 76*(5), 47–58.

Hitt, M. A., & Tyler, B. B. (1991). Strategic decision models: Integrating different perspectives. *Strategic Management Journal, 12*, 327–351.

Hodgkinson, G. P., Sadler-Smith, E., Burke, L. A., Claxton, G., & Sparrow, P. R. (2009). Intuition in organizations: Implications for strategic management. *Long Range Planning, 42*, 277–297.

Hogarth, R. M., & Makridakis, S. (1981). The value of decision making in a complex environment: An experimental approach. *Management Science, 27*, 93–107.

Hough, J. R., & Ogilvie, D. (2005). An empirical test of cognitive style and strategic decision outcomes. *Journal of Management Studies, 42*, 417–448.

Hristov, I., Camilli, R., & Mechelli, A. (2022). Cognitive biases in implementing a performance management system: Behavioral strategy for supporting managers' decision-making processes. *Management Research Review, 45*(9), 1110–1136.

Hunt, R. G., Krzystofiak, F. J., Meindl, J. R., & Yousry, A. M. (1989). Cognitive style and decision making. *Organizational Behavior and Human Decision Processes, 44*(3), 436–453.

Intezari, A., & Gressel, S. (2017). Information and reformation in KM systems: Big data and strategic decision-making. *Journal of Knowledge Management, 21*(1), 71–91.

James, H., & Barnes, J. R. (1984). Cognitive biases and their impact on strategic planning. *Strategic Management Journal, 5*(2), 129–137.

Janssen, M., Voort, H., & Wahyudi, A. (2017). Factors influencing big data decision-making quality. *Journal of Business Research, 70*, 338–345.

Kahneman, D., Slovic, P., & Tversky, A. (1982). *Judgment under uncertainty: Heuristics and biases.* Cambridge University Press.

Keh, H. T., Foo, M., & Lim, B. C. (2002). Opportunity evaluation under risky conditions: The cognitive processes of entrepreneurs. *Entrepreneurship: Theory and Practice, 27*(2), 125–148.

Khatri, N., & Ng, H. A. (2000). The role of intuition in strategic decision making. *Human Relations, 53*(1), 57–86.

Knight, D., Pearce, C. L., Smith, K. G., Olian, J. D., Sims, H. P., Smith, K. A., & Flood, P. (1999). Top management team diversity, group process, and strategic consensus. *Strategic Management Journal, 20*(5), 445–465.

Korteling, J. E., & Toet, A. (2020). Cognitive biases. In S., Della Sala (Ed.), *Encyclopedia of behavioral neuroscience* (vol. 3, pp. 610–619). Elsevier.

Kubra Canhilal, S., Lepori, B., & Seeber, M. (2016). Decision-making power and institutional logic in higher education institutions: A comparative analysis of European universities. In *Towards a comparative institutionalism: Forms, dynamics and logics across the organizational fields of health care and higher education* (Vol. 45, pp. 169–194). Emerald Group Publishing Limited.

Liu, F., & Maitlis, S. (2014). Emotional dynamics and strategizing processes: A study of strategic conversations in top team meetings. *Journal of Management Studies, 51*(2), 202–234.

Lounsbury, M. (2007). A tale of two cities: Competing logics and practice variation in the professionalizing of mutual funds. *Academy of Management Journal, 50*(2), 289–307.

Maitlis, S. (2005). The social processes of organizational sensemaking. *Academy of Management Journal, 48*(1), 21–49.

March, J. G., & Shapira, Z. (1987). Managerial perspectives on risk and risk taking. *Management Science, 33*(11), 1404–1418.

March, J. G., & Simon, H. A. (1958). *Organizations.* John Wiley & Sons.

Merendino, A., Dibb, S., Meadows, M., Quinn, L., Wilson, D., Simkin, L., & Canhoto, A. (2018). Big data, big decisions: The impact of big data on board level decision-making. *Journal of Business Research, 93*, 67–78.

Meyer, J. W., & Rowan, B. (1977). Institutionalized organizations: Formal structure as myth and ceremony. *American Journal of Sociology, 83*(2), 340–363.

Miller, C. C., Burke, L. M., & Glick, W. H. (1998). Cognitive diversity among upper-echelon executives: Implications for strategic decision processes. *Strategic Management Journal, 19*(1), 39–58.

Miller, C. C., & Ireland, R. D. (2005). Intuition in strategic decision making: Friend or foe in the fast-paced 21st century? *Academy of Management Perspectives, 19*, 19–30.

Neisser, U. (1967). *Cognitive psychology.* Appleton-Century-Crofts.

North, D. C. (1991). *Institutions, Institutional change and economic performance.* Cambridge University Press.

Ocasio, W. (1999). Institutionalized action and corporate governance: The reliance on rules of CEO succession. *Administrative Science Quarterly, 44*(2), 384–416.

Oliver, C. (1990). Determinants of interorganizational relationships: Integration and future directions. *Academy of Management Review, 15*(2), 241–265.

Oliver, C. (1991). Strategic responses to institutional processes. *The Academy of Management Review, 16*(1), 145–179.

Oliver, C. (1997). Sustainable competitive advantage: Combining institutional and resource-based views. *Strategic Management Journal, 18*(9), 697–713.

Olson, B. J., Parayitam, S., & Bao, Y. (2007). Strategic decision making: The effects of cognitive diversity, conflict, and trust on decision outcomes. *Journal of Management, 33*(2), 196–222.

Pache, A. C., & Santos, F. (2010). When worlds collide: The internal dynamics of organizational responses to conflicting institutional demands. *Academy of Management Review, 35,* 455–476.

Pache, A. C., & Santos, F. (2013). Inside the hybrid organization: Selective coupling as a response to competing institutional logics. *Academy of Management Journal, 56,* 972–1001.

Papadakis, V., & Barwise, P. (1997). Research on strategic decisions: Where do we go from here? In V. Papadakis, & P. Barwise (Eds.), *Strategic decisions* (pp. 289–302). Kluwer Academic Publishers.

Pauleen, D. J., & Wang, W. Y. (2017). Does big data mean big knowledge? KM perspectives on big data and analytics. *Journal of Knowledge Management, 21*(1), 1–6.

Peng, M. (2002). Towards an institution-based view of business strategy. *Asia Pacific Journal of Management, 19*(2–3), 251–267.

Peng, M. W., Sun, S. L., Pinkham, B., & Chen, H. (2009). The institution-based view as a third leg for a strategy tripod. *The Academy of Management Perspectives, 23*(3), 63–81.

Plessner, H., Betsch, C., & Betsch, T. (2011). *Intuition in judgment and decision making.* Taylor & Francis.

Quinn, J. B. (1980). *Strategies for change: Logical incrementalism.* Richard D Irwin.

Reeves, M., Goodson, B., & Whitaker, K. (2021). The power of anomaly: To achieve strategic advantage, scan the market for surprises. *Harvard Business Review.* July–Aug.

Sadler-Smith, E., & Shefy, E. (2004). The intuitive executive: Understanding and applying "gut feel" in decision-making. *Political Research Quarterly, 44,* 762–783.

Schwenk, C. R. (1984). Cognitive simplification processes in strategic decision-making. *Strategic management journal, 5*(2), 111–128.

Schwenk, C. H. (1986). Information, cognitive biases, and commitment to a course of action. *Academy of Management Review, 11*(2), 298–310.

Seidl, D. (2004). The concept of weak signals revisited: A re-description from a constructivist perspective. In H. Tsoukas & J. Shepherd (Eds.), *Managing the future: Developing foresight in the knowledge economy* (pp. 153–170). Blackwell.

Shapira, Z. (1995). Risk taking: A managerial perspective. Russell Sage Foundation.

Shrivastava, P., & Grant, J. H. (1985). Empirically derived models of strategic decision-making processes. *Strategic Management Journal, 6*(2), 97–113.

Simon, H. A. (1947). *Administrative behavior.* The Free Press.

Simon, H. A. (1957). Models of man; social and rational. Wiley.

Simon, M., Houghton, S. M., & Aquino, K. (2000). Cognitive biases, risk perception, and venture formation: How individuals decide to start companies. *Journal of Business Venturing, 15*(2), 113–134.

Smith, W. K., Gonin, M., & Besharov, M. L. (2013). Managing social-business tensions: A review and research agenda for social enterprise. *Business Ethics Quarterly*, *23*, 407–442.

Sorrell, M., Komisar, R., & Mulcahy, A. (2010). How we do it: Three executives reflect on strategic decision making. *McKinsey Quarterly*, *2*, 46–57.

Stubbart, C. I. (1989). Managerial cognition: A missing link in strategic management research. *Journal of Management Studies*, *26*, 325–347.

Teixeira, M. G., De Déa Roglio, K., & Marcon, R. (2017). Institutional logics and the decision-making process of adopting corporate governance at a cooperative organization. *Journal of Management & Governance*, *21*, 181–209.

Thornton, P. H., Jones, C., & Kury, K. (2005). Institutional logics and institutional change in organizations: Transformation in accounting, architecture, and publishing. In *Transformation in cultural industries* (pp. 125–170). Emerald Group Publishing Limited.

Thornton, P. H., & Ocasio, W. (1999). Institutional logics and the historical contingency of power in organizations: Executive succession in the higher education publishing industry, 1958–1990. *American Journal of Sociology*, *105*, 801–843.

Thornton, P. H., & Ocasio, W. (2008). Institutional logics. In R., Greenwood, C., Oliver, R., Suddaby, & K. Sahlin, (Eds). *The Sage handbook of organizational institutionalism* (vol. 840, 99–128). SAGE Publications Ltd, https://doi.org/10.4135/9781849200387

Thornton, P. H., Ocasio, W., & Lounsbury, M. (2012). *The institutional logics perspective*. John Wiley & Sons, Inc.

Vassilis, M. P., Spyros, L., & David, C. (1998). Strategic decision-making processes: The role of management and context. *Strategic Management Journal*, *19*, 115–147.

Vidgen, R., Shaw, S., & Grant, D. B. (2017). Management challenges in creating value from business analytics. *European Journal of Operational Research*, *261*(2), 626–639.

Von Groddeck, V., & Schwarz, J. O. (2013). Perceiving megatrends as empty signifiers: A discourse-theoretical interpretation of trend management. *Futures*, *47*, 28–37.

Wang, H., Xu, Z., Fujita, H., & Liu, S. (2016). Towards felicitous decision making: An overview on challenges and trends of big data. *Information Sciences*, *367*, 747–765.

Whittington, R. (2001). The practice of strategy: Theoretical resources and empirical possibilities. Proceedings of the EIASM Workshop on Micro Strategy and Strategising, Brussels, Belgium, 1–3 February, 2001.

Wiersema, M. F., & Bantel, K. A. (1992). Top management team demography and corporate strategic change. *Academy of Management Journal*, *35*(1), 91–121.

Woiceshyn, J. (2009). Lessons from "good minds": How CEOs use intuition, analysis and guiding principles to make strategic decisions. *Long Range Planning*, *42*(3), 298–319.

Yan, S., Ferraro, F., & Almandoz, J. (2019). The rise of socially responsible investment funds: The paradoxical role of the financial logic. *Administrative Science Quarterly*, *64*(2), 466–501. https://doi.org/10.1177/0001839218773324

4 Leadership and Transformation

Chiara Acciarini, Paolo Boccardelli,
and Federica Brunetta

4.1 Introduction

As introduced in the previous chapters, the managerial landscape has undergone a seismic shift, placing leaders in the eye of a storm characterized by unparalleled complexity, volatility, and ambiguity. This tumultuous environment has presented an exigent challenge, compelling managers to rapidly recalibrate their decision-making frameworks, interrogate established leadership paradigms, and reimagine their organizational vision and strategies. The convergence of megatrends and transformative forces has wielded a profound influence, reshaping the fundamental architecture of business models, operational processes, and the very fabric of organizational structures. This upheaval has not merely prompted a reconsideration of current paradigms; it has also set the stage for a new approach aimed at navigating and capitalizing on future waves of change.

In the face of transformations, complexities, and uncertainties, leaders need to be ready to seize opportunities. This chapter focuses on strategic change and the role of managers – and leaders – in navigating and steering that change through Strategic Decision-Making, Planning, and Implementation. Leadership in the face of transformation demands a mastery of dynamic managerial capabilities to navigate the multifaceted changes. This involves not just adapting to these metamorphoses but also harnessing them as facilitators for growth. It necessitates awareness of the shifting waves of the market, enabling leaders to recalibrate their organizations' corporate strategies. This recalibration involves a strategic realignment, a process that optimizes the existing framework, capitalizing on nascent opportunities, and fortifying against potential threats.

To this end, the chapter also focuses on transformative leadership, which has emerged in management literature as a compelling approach that goes beyond traditional management practices, involving inspiring and empowering individuals and teams to reach their full potential, fostering a shared vision, and driving positive change. As transformative leaders, new managers should develop and leverage specific qualities to be effective at both the micro and

DOI: 10.4324/9781003459804-4

macro levels and as decision-makers. Finally, the chapter examines the relevance of remote leadership in the age of digitalization.

4.2   Vision and Strategic Change

Various scholars have put forth different perspectives on strategic change (e.g. Boeker, 1989; Choi et al., 2021; Fiss & Zajac, 2006; Gioia & Chittipeddi, 1991; Hofer & Schendel, 1978; Rajagopalan & Spreitzer, 1997; Romanelli & Tushman, 1994; Tushman & Romanelli, 1985; Van de Ven & Poole, 1995; Zhang & Rajagopalan, 2010).

Some definitions describe strategic change as a significant transformation or reorientation in a company's existence (Romanelli & Tushman, 1994; Tushman & Romanelli, 1985), while others interpret strategic change as a shift toward prioritizing shareholder value (Fiss & Zajac, 2006) or as an alteration in cognitive and behavioral patterns (Gioia & Chittipeddi, 1991). Westphal and Fredrickson (2001) have highlighted the strategic change of a firm as a useful approach to determine new corporate strategies to compete in evolving contexts. Indeed, strategizing is not a simple process but rather entails micro-level processes within organizations and across different players that are actively engaged in constructing and executing strategies (Maitlis & Lawrence, 2003; Whittington, 1996, 2001) and that influence an organization's capability to plan and execute strategies.

Generally, strategic change entails substantial modifications in resources to adapt to environmental conditions and uncertainties (Carpenter, 2000; Choi et al., 2021; Hofer & Schendel, 1978; Rajagopalan & Spreitzer, 1997; Tushman & Romanelli, 1985; Van de Ven & Poole, 1995). Scholars have found that strategic change can enhance a firm's chances of survival (Fiss & Zajac, 2006; Haveman, 1992; Romanelli & Tushman, 1994; Smith & Grimm, 1987; Tushman & Romanelli, 1985; Zajac et al., 2000) or its performance (Smith & Grimm, 1987; Zajac & Kraatz, 1993) in the event of profound shifts in environmental conditions. Nonetheless, other studies have also examined the negative effects of strategic change (Naranjo-Gil et al., 2008; Zajac & Kraatz, 1993). Accordingly, extant research has focused on the effects of atypical performance outcomes, not only in terms of success, but also in terms of failure. This has allowed for a greater understanding of how organizations learn from past experiences, and more specifically, from very positive (success) or very negative (recovery) experiences that are distinct in nature from other types of outcomes and may change strategic decision-making routines (e.g. Kim et al., 2009).

In today's constantly evolving business environment, change is inevitable. As organizations strive to remain competitive, they must continuously adapt their strategies to keep pace with shifting market demands, new technologies, and changing customer preferences. This requires leaders to have a clear vision to navigate the challenges and uncertainties ahead. In other words, it is crucial to fully understand the company's current position as well as the ability to envision a future state that is both desirable and achievable. According to Morris (1987), strategic vision implies a profound environmental scanning ability, and it serves as a powerful tool for driving change and providing a shared sense of purpose and direction across the organization. For instance, by articulating a vision of the future, leaders can move their employees to think differently and embrace new ways of working.

This requires a systematic approach to plan and implement new corporate strategies by including a thorough analysis of the competitive environment, along with an assessment of the organization's strengths, weaknesses, opportunities, and threats. For instance, the preliminary results of research conducted by Acciarini and Boccardelli (2024, working paper) show that the more dynamic the environmental conditions, the higher the probability of M&As, strategic alliances, and joint ventures, along with the implementation of product and geographic diversification.

To sum up, vision and strategic planning are closely intertwined. A strong vision provides the foundation for developing a strategic plan that aligns the organization's resources and capabilities with its goals and objectives. The organizational response to novel problems, complexities, and trends – or disruptions – lies in the enactment of strategic decision-making processes, which are the responsibility of top management and account for both internal context and logics, as well as external scenarios (Alexiev et al., 2010; Clark & Maggitti, 2012; Dean & Sharfman, 1993; Elbanna, 2006; Hickson et al., 1986; Ireland & Miller, 2004; Mintzberg et al., 1976; Pettigrew, 1992; Schwenk, 1988; Shrivastava & Grant, 1985). Strategic decisions imply "committing substantial resources, setting precedents, and creating waves of lesser decisions (Mintzberg et al., 1976); as ill-structured, non-routine and complex (Schwenk, 1988); and as substantial, unusual and all pervading (Hickson et al., 1986)" (Dean & Sharfman, 1993; pp. 379–380). Research on strategic decision-making (Alexiev et al., 2010; Clark & Maggitti, 2012; Dean & Sharfman, 1993; Elbanna, 2006; Hickson et al., 1986; Ireland & Miller, 2004; Mintzberg et al., 1976; Pettigrew, 1992; Schwenk, 1988; Shrivastava & Grant, 1985) has focused on the content of decisions, such as new product or new market development, growth direction, divestment, competitive tactics, operations, etc. (Alexiev et al., 2010; Kandemir & Acur, 2012; Moenaert et al., 2010), and on the processes, focusing on the ratio, drivers, and factors affecting decisions that have the potential to change the strategic direction (Eisenhardt & Zbaracki, 1992; Elbanna, 2006; Pettigrew, 1992).

So, the decision to change strategy requires a comprehensive examination of the firm's context, as well as external scenarios, along with a willingness to invest in new capabilities and resources that are required to achieve the vision. This may involve divesting or restructuring existing operations, as well as developing new products or markets (Håkanson & Kappen, 2017; Kandemir & Acur, 2012) or reconfiguring existing business models.

4.3   Dynamic Capabilities and Traits of Leaders

Nowadays, leaders must manage ever more crises and take on innovation to shape sustainable strategies. Environmental transformations like technological progress or the 2008 financial crisis threaten normal business activities and force leaders to consider these changes as a "new normal" by adapting the firm's corporate strategies. Organizational adaptation after change, jolts, or failures seems to be common to many successful organizations (e.g. Kim et al., 2009; Maitlis & Lawrence, 2003). Most CEOs believe they will need to change their business models in the next three years, while half report they are currently changing their business models (Freakley, 2023). This means that this type of leadership challenge is unprecedented. The exploration of why managers modify and tailor a firm's resource and competences base to align with changing conditions has been a central area of study in the field of dynamic management capabilities since the influential research conducted by Adner and Helfat (2003). Their work built upon the dynamic capabilities framework introduced by Teece et al. (1997).

Broadly speaking, these capabilities empower firms to adapt and adjust their resources and competences, allowing them to initiate strategic changes in response to changes within the business scenario (Dixon et al., 2014; Schilke et al., 2018). While leaders who possess ordinary capabilities are essential to various aspects of the organization – such as efficient manufacturing processes, effective marketing strategies, and valuable partnerships – the presence of dynamic capabilities is crucial to identify novel products and services, thereby potentially revealing untapped markets where competitors have yet to emerge. Therefore, dynamic managerial capabilities can be considered the type of abilities necessary to manage and adapt to the transformations occurring in the external context, and they allow leaders to make the most of new opportunities by reconfiguring the existing firm's corporate strategies.

According to Teece (2007), dynamic capabilities can be categorized into three types: sensing, seizing, and reconfiguring. Sensing involves the identification of changes in the environment, seizing refers to the opportunity to take advantage of these changes, and reconfiguring encompasses the possible reorganization of resources and capabilities of firms to exploit these opportunities. Effective leadership is crucial for the development of dynamic capabilities, and leaders play a central role in the sensing, seizing, and reconfiguring processes of these competences. For instance, in the sensing process, leaders need to be able to pick up on new trends and transformations and to understand the effect of these changes on firms. In the seizing process, since large amounts of data are available in the market, leaders should be able to gather, analyze, and interpret it properly to make informed decisions. Finally, in the reconfiguring process, leaders need to be able to reallocate and reconfigure the resources and capabilities of the firm to exploit the various opportunities that arise from new disruptive transformations. In addition to being able to develop new skills and knowledge, another important challenge concerns the ability to integrate additional external resources and capabilities into existing ones.

In recent years, the transformation of corporate leadership requires that guidance be more collaborative, active, communicative, and flexible with the structural changes that occur.

Over the past decade, scholars have debated about the relationship between individual traits of leaders and the outcomes of leadership, and developed taxonomies linking traits, antecedents, and outcomes (e.g. Fleishman & Mumford, 1991; Mumford et al., 2000; Zaccaro et al., 2004, 2018).

Scholars have focused on personality traits (Judge & Long, 2012), leadership styles (Judge et al., 2009), skills and abilities (Antonakis, 2011; Judge et al., 2009; Zaccaro et al., 2018), emotional intelligence (Antonakis, 2011; Judge et al., 2009; Tuncdogan et al., 2017; Zaccaro et al., 2018) or even "bright" and "dark" traits of leaders (Judge et al., 2009).

Indeed, the term "trait" has generated confusion over time, as it has been used to describe diverse qualities of individuals, ranging from personality to behavior, abilities, and even physical or demographic attributes, which can be abstracted from situational contingencies (Zaccaro et al., 2004). As recognized by Amabile et al. (2004), the concept of leadership appears significantly influenced by ever-changing dynamics and related to factors like societal, environmental characteristics, culture and ethics, institutional factors, organizational values, and strategies.

The first relevant characteristic that a leader must possess is *vision*, which is also the starting point of the journey toward the firm's success. In particular, the ability to understand the potential of a specific internal or external action or resource, identifying the path to be taken to achieve the goals, and finally, the involvement of teams and various stakeholders. These factors represent the core skills for corporate leadership. After defining the firm's needs, one should implement a *creative thinking process* aimed at experimenting and inspiring ideas and innovation, and then providing the right motivation to the entire organization.

To this end, Bill Klemm, in the book *Leadership Today* (Klemm, 2017), identifies four categories of fundamental principles that each successful leader should follow:

1 Change of emotional and cognitive state, which includes the managerial ability to frame a problem by adopting a different perspective;
2 Change of physical properties, which can be implemented, for example, through visual representation of elements or through the correlation of things and situations;

3 Comparison, which materializes in the identification of possible solutions connected to a specific problem; and
4 Reconstruction and deconstruction, in which ideas are initially broken down and then recombined.

The strategy *execution* is essential for the entire process, as well: according to an MIT Sloan Management Review report, the most high-performing companies are those that have invested the most time, energy, and money into strategy implementation (Kane et al., 2017). Therefore, the real distinctive strength of an organization lies in its ability to react promptly to changes by taking opportunities through the development of a business that must be constantly reconsidered, updated, and innovated. Finally, the *impact* phase concerns how planned and implemented actions effectively influence people, organizations, and society at large.

4.4 Transformative and Remote Leadership

As previously discussed, in today's dynamic environment, leaders are faced with challenges in guiding their organizations toward growth and sustainability. Transformative leadership has emerged as a compelling approach that goes beyond traditional management practices. At its core, transformative leadership involves inspiring and empowering individuals and teams to reach their full potential, fostering a shared vision, and driving positive change. In this sense, transformative leaders promote collaboration, cultivate trust, prioritize the development of their employees, and contribute to generating social impact.

Transformative leadership represents a morally grounded model that prioritizes the enduring welfare of stakeholders and society while honoring the ethical responsibilities of organizations toward their stakeholders (Ciulla et al., 2005). Thus, by embodying the highest standards of moral guidance, these types of leaders amplify the commitment of followers (Caldwell & Hayes, 2007; Senge, 2006) while achieving exceptional standards (Hosmer, 2007; Kouzes & Posner, 2010; Solomon, 1992).

The credibility of leadership is a product of leaders merging competence and character; both attributes are indispensable, with neither solely sufficient (Covey, 2004). In other words, across extensive leadership inquiries, a leader's unwavering dedication to integrity emerges as the pivotal element for establishing personal credibility (Kouzes & Posner, 2010).

According to the World Economic Forum (Wagner, 2020), new leaders should be curious, resilient, collaborative, and flexible to properly navigate the current uncertainty and volatility. Firms that face external transformation need leaders who leverage their curiosity to foster a culture of innovation to encourage experimentation and embrace failure as a learning opportunity. These types of leaders, therefore, create platforms for idea generation, facilitate cross-functional collaboration, and provide resources to support and implement innovative initiatives. The new leadership approach also requires that resilience be developed to preserve a positive mindset and a sense of opportunity in times of change (Folkman, 2017).

Moreover, leaders who are collaborative tend to build strong connections with their teams, colleagues, and stakeholders at large. They invest time in understanding the needs, aspirations, and concerns of individuals, fostering a feeling of inclusion and loyalty across the organization. By creating a collaborative environment, transformative leaders foster diverse thinking and enable collective problem-solving. In other words, these kinds of leaders recognize that their success lies in the creation of a supportive environment inspiring individuals to make decisions and to contribute with their unique perspective. Finally, adapting to a rapidly changing environment is a determinant skill that allows companies to develop innovative business models and maintain their competitive advantage.

Given the increasing emphasis on sustainability and the accountability of leaders for both their own decisions and those of others, they can significantly amplify their positive impact by establishing an inclusive environment (Bazerman, 2020). In fact, authenticity and integrity are foundational characteristics of transformative leaders who lead by example, demonstrating consistency between their words and actions. A recent survey shows that most companies living in a reshaped world need more moral leaders at the helm and that moral leadership would drive business performance (Seidman, 2021). Thus, by embodying transparency, honesty, and ethical behavior, new leaders establish a culture of trust and accountability within their organization, and they are central in the creation of most of the value for society.

Of the various transformations discussed, digital transformation has completely changed the face of entire markets and economies. As technology continues to advance, the concept of remote work has gained widespread acceptance and popularity. After the COVID-19 pandemic, on a global scale, 68% of employees showed a preference for a hybrid work schedule, while around 25% of them indicated a desire for entirely remote work (Wood, 2022). With regard to the age groups, young employees believed that 100% homeworking was more beneficial to effective collaboration than hybrid or office-based work; instead, senior leaders considered that collaboration peaked in an office setting (Wood, 2022). Nowadays, approximately 26% of employees engage in remote work, and it is projected that 36.2 million workers will do so by 2025 (Zippia, 2022). Business leaders are increasingly tasked with the challenge of managing and inspiring teams that are geographically dispersed. In fact, the new workplace is characterized by employees who operate outside of a traditional office environment and who adopt advanced communication tools and flexible work arrangements.

The proliferation of remote work in recent years, accelerated by technological advancements and global circumstances, has revolutionized the concept of leadership. As teams become increasingly distributed across various locations, the role of remote leadership has emerged as a critical factor in organizational success. Of course, remote work offers multiple advantages, such as heightened performance and productivity, stronger engagement, and easier talent retention (Farrer, 2020). However, it also presents unique challenges, including communication barriers, lack of face-to-face interaction, potential feelings of isolation, and difficulties in maintaining team cohesion. For example, effective communication is particularly critical in remote teams where leaders should establish regular check-ins, encourage video conferencing whenever possible, and foster an open-door policy to facilitate information sharing. In addition, since communication lies at the heart of successful remote leadership, these leaders should foster open channels of communication by encouraging active listening and by establishing regular feedback sessions to maintain alignment and clarity among team members.

Leading remote teams characterized by adaptability, collaboration, and a positive atmosphere is recognized as a hallmark of success for remote leaders. Team culture encompasses the responsibilities, competencies, mindsets, and perspectives within a collective of employees. For instance, agile teams prioritize collaborative efforts and continual growth (Li et al., 2016). Moreover, promoting flexibility in roles and establishing shared objectives contributes positively to team morale, indirectly impacting overall outcomes (Li et al., 2016; Verburg et al., 2013).

Research by Hahm (2017) highlights the advantageous impact of fostering a culture of sharing information dissemination within teams, consequently enhancing innovation and creativity. Additionally, a positive team culture has the potential to inspire members, aligning with Goh and Wasko's (2012) findings that attribute improved group assignments and individual autonomy to enhanced member performance. Taylor et al. (2013) suggest that in remote teams, intermediate technology proficiency might enhance employee satisfaction with remote relationships.

In general, remote leaders should actively promote and recognize remote work as a valued and integral part of the organization. Achieving this involves offering training and resources specifically tailored to remote employees, facilitating virtual team-building activities, and celebrating distant team achievements. In the digital business context, remote leaders actively promote collaboration among employees, encourage idea-sharing, engage with customers, and facilitate real-time connections across functions or geographical areas. To do this, they leverage remote tools, such as remote conferencing, collaborative whiteboard tools, forums and live chats, and additional project management and collaboration tools to enhance communication efficiency and efficacy. However, distant communication can be challenging and less impactful compared to face-to-face interactions. For this reason, in interacting with their stakeholders and in order to be successful, remote leaders should also possess a high level of self-awareness, social and emotional intelligence, and empathy that other types of leaders may lack (Landry, 2019).

Finally, trust holds considerable importance in leadership, and researchers have extensively investigated various factors contributing to its formation (Dirks & Ferrin, 2002; Kramer & Tyler, 1996). Studies exploring the impact of previous relationships within proximal and virtual teams indicate that existing competencies and knowledge significantly influence the development of trust, subsequent performance, and member satisfaction (Alge et al., 2003). For instance, even a single in-person meeting among members of virtual teams, may establish a prior link, and has been recognized as a potential for heightened team effectiveness (Kelley & Kelloway, 2012).

4.5 Conclusions

In this chapter, we started by defining the relevance of strategic change within the strategy and organizational context, highlighting the multiple perspectives that have been provided in managerial literature. Because the current business scenario is characterized by complexity, volatility, and ambiguity, effective strategic decision-making requires a link between innovative and transformative leadership aligned with strategic vision, creativity, effective strategy execution, and adaptability.

Indeed, the ability and willingness of leaders to invest in new capabilities and resources is required to achieve *vision* and come up with a strategy. In this light, leaders must possess characteristics and abilities to navigate environmental transformations and reconfigure strategies to make the most of new opportunities so that dynamic managerial capabilities become crucial in adapting to change, seizing opportunities, and reshaping corporate strategies.

The chapter has also underlined the way transformative leaders are able to go beyond traditional management practices, fostering collaboration, innovation, and inclusivity within teams and organizations. Additionally, the chapter accounted for critical issues that have arisen as part of digital transformation and delved into the benefits (e.g. increased productivity and flexibility) and the challenges posed by remote leadership, and the crucial role of communication, emotional intelligence, and adaptability. To sum up, the new business landscape requires adaptable and innovative leaders, possessing the strategic vision, adaptability, transformative leadership practices, and remote leadership strategies to navigate uncertainties and guide effective strategic change.

References

Acciarini, C., & Boccardelli, P. (2024) *The impact of environmental dynamism and board digital expertise on the method and scope of a firm's strategic change.* Working paper.

Adner, R., & Helfat, C. E. (2003). Corporate effects and dynamic managerial capabilities. *Strategic Management Journal, 24*(10), 1011–1025.

Alexiev, A. S., Jansen, J. J., Van den Bosch, F. A., & Volberda, H. W. (2010). Top management team advice seeking and exploratory innovation: The moderating role of TMT heterogeneity. *Journal of Management Studies, 47*(7), 1343–1364.

Alge, B. J., Wiethoff, C., & Klein, H. J. (2003). When does the medium matter? Knowledge-building experiences and opportunities in decision-making teams. *Organizational Behavior and Human Decision Processes, 91*, 26–37.

Amabile, T. M., Schatzel, E. A., Moneta, G. B., & Kramer, S. J. (2004). Leader behaviors and the work environment for creativity: Perceived leader support. *The Leadership Quarterly, 15*(1), 5–32

Antonakis, J. (2011). Predictors of leadership: The usual suspects and the suspect traits. In A. Bryman, D. Collinson, K. Grint, B. Jackson, & M. Uhl-Bien (Eds). *Sage handbook of leadership.* (pp. 269–285). Sage Publications.

Bazerman, M. H. (2020). A new model for ethical leadership. *Harvard Business Review, 98*(5) (September–October 2020): 90–97.

Boeker, W. (1989). Strategic change: The effects of founding and history. *Academy of Management Journal, 32*(3), 489–515.

Caldwell, C., & Hayes, L. (2007). Leadership, trustworthiness, and the mediating lens. *Journal of Management Development, 26*(3), 261–278.

Carpenter, M. A. (2000). The price of change: The role of CEO compensation in strategic variation and deviation from industry strategy norms. *Journal of Management, 26*(6), 1179–1198.

Choi, S., Liu, H., Yin, J., Qi, Y., & Lee, J. Y. (2021). The effect of political turnover on firms' strategic change in the emerging economies: The moderating role of political connections and financial resources. *Journal of Business Research, 137*, 255–266.

Ciulla, J. B., Price, T. L., & Murphy, S. E. (2005). *The quest for moral leaders: Essays on leadership ethics.* Edward Elgar.

Clark, K. D., & Maggitti, P. G. (2012). TMT potency and strategic decision-making in high technology firms. *Journal of Management Studies, 49*(7), 1168–1193.

Covey, S. R. (2004). *The 8th habit: From effectiveness to greatness.* Free Press.

Dean, J. W., & Sharfman, M. P. (1993). The relationship between procedural rationality and political behavior in strategic decision making. *Decision Sciences, 24*(6), 1069–1083.

Dirks, K. T., & Ferrin, D. L. (2002). Trust in leadership: Meta-analytic findings and implications for research and practice. *Journal of Applied Psychology, 87*, 611–628.

Dixon, S., Meyer, K., & Day, M. (2014). Building dynamic capabilities of adaptation and innovation: A study of micro-foundations in a transition economy. *Long Range Planning, 47*(4), 186–205.

Eisenhardt, K. M., & Zbaracki, M. J. (1992). Strategic decision making. *Strategic Management Journal, 13*(S2), 17–37.

Elbanna, S. (2006). Strategic decision-making: Process perspectives. *International Journal of Management Reviews, 8*(1), 1–20.

Farrer, L. (2020). *5 Proven Benefits of Remote Work for Companies.* https://www.forbes.com/sites/laurelfarrer/2020/02/12/top-5-benefits-of-remote-work-for-companies/?sh=7dc7c0b416c8

Fiss, P. C., & Zajac, E. J. (2006). The symbolic management of strategic change: Sensegiving via framing and decoupling. *Academy of Management Journal, 49*(6), 1173–1193.

Fleishman, E. A., & Mumford, M. D. (1991). Evaluating classifications of job behavior: A construct validation of the ability requirement scales. *Personnel Psychology, 44*(3), 523–575.

Folkman, J. (2017). *New Research: 7 Ways to Become a More Resilient Leader.* https://www.forbes.com/sites/joefolkman/2017/04/06/new-research-7-ways-to-become-a-more-resilient-leader/?sh=737689da7a0c

Freakley, S. (2023). *Disruption may be the new economic driver: Here's how leaders can meet the challenge.* World Economic Forum.

Gioia, D. A., & Chittipeddi, K. (1991). Sensemaking and sensegiving in strategic change initiation. *Strategic Management Journal, 12*(6), 433–448.

Goh, S., & Wasko, M. (2012). The effects of leader-member exchange on member performance in virtual world teams. *Journal of the Association of Information Systems, 13*(10), 861–885. doi: 10.17705/1jais.00308.

Hahm, S. (2017). Information sharing and creativity in a virtual team: Roles of authentic leadership, sharing team climate and psychological empowerment. *KSII Transactions on Internet and Information Systems, 11*(8), 4105–4119.

Håkanson, L., & Kappen, P. (2017). The "Casino Model" of internationalization: An alternative Uppsala paradigm. *Journal of International Business Studies, 48*, 1103–1113.

Haveman, H. A. (1992). Between a rock and a hard place: Organizational change and performance under conditions of fundamental environmental transformation. *Administrative Science Quarterly*, 37(1): 48–75.

Hickson, D. J., Butler, R. J., Cray, D., Mallory, G. R., & Wilson, D. C. (1986). *Top decisions: Strategic decision-making in organizations.* Basil Blackwell.

Hofer, C. W., & Schendel, D. (1978). *Strategy formulation: Analytical concepts.* West Publishing.

Hosmer, L. T. (2007). *The ethics of management* (6th ed.). McGraw-Hill.

Ireland, R. D., & Miller, C. C. (2004). Decision-making and firm success. *Academy of Management Perspectives, 18*(4), 8–12.

Judge, T. A., & Long, D. M. (2012). Individual differences in leadership. *The Nature of Leadership, 2*, 179–217.

Judge, T. A., Piccolo, R. F., & Kosalka, T. (2009). The bright and dark sides of leader traits: A review and theoretical extension of the leader trait paradigm. *The Leadership Quarterly, 20*(6), 855–875.

Kandemir, D., & Acur, N. (2012). Examining proactive strategic decision-making flexibility in new product development. *Journal of Product Innovation Management, 29*(4), 608–622.

Kane, G. C., Palmer, D., Phillips, A. N., Kiron, D., & Buckley, N. (2017). Achieving digital maturity. *MIT Sloan Management Review*. 59(1), 1–32.

Kelley, E., & Kelloway, E. K. (2012). Context matters: Testing a model of remote leadership. *Journal of Leadership & Organizational Studies, 19*(4), 437–449. doi: 10.1177/1548051812454173.

Kim, J.-Y., Kim, J.-Y., & Miner, A. S. (2009). Organizational learning from extreme performance experience: The impact of success and recovery experience. *Organization Science, 20*(6), 958–978.

Klemm, W. (2017). Leadership and creativity. Springer Texts in Business and Economics, In Joan Marques & Satinder Dhiman (Eds.), *Leadership today: Practices for personal and professional performance* (Chapter 15, pp. 263–278). Springer.

Kouzes, J. M., & Posner, B. Z. (2010). *The leadership challenge: How to keep getting extraordinary things done in organizations* (4th ed.). Pfeiffer.

Kramer, R. M., & Tyler, T. R. (Eds.). (1996). *Trust in organizations*. SAGE.

Landry, L. (2019). Why emotional intelligence is important in leadership. Harvard Business School. https://online.hbs.edu/blog/post/emotional-intelligence-in-leadership

Li, W., Liu, K., Belitski, M., Ghobadian, A., & O'Regan, N. (2016). E-leadership through strategic alignment: An empirical study of small- and medium-sized enterprises in the digital age. *Journal of Information Technology, 31*(2), 185–206.

Maitlis, S., & Lawrence, T. B. (2003). Orchestral manoeuvres in the dark: Understanding failure in organizational strategizing. *Available at SSRN 371247.*

Mintzberg, H., Raisinghani, D., & Theoret, A. (1976). The structure of "unstructured" decision processes. *Administrative Science Quarterly*, 21(2), 246–275.

Moenaert, R. K., Robben, H., Antioco, M., De Schamphelaere, V., & Roks, E. (2010). Strategic innovation decisions: What you foresee is not what you get. *Journal of Product Innovation Management, 27*(6), 840–855.

Morris, E. (1987). Vision and strategy: A focus for the future. *Journal of Business Strategy, 8*(2), 51–58.

Mumford, M. D., Zaccaro, S. J., Harding, F. D., Jacobs, T. O., & Fleishman, E. A. (2000). Leadership skills for a changing world: Solving complex social problems. *The Leadership Quarterly, 11*(1), 11–35.

Naranjo-Gil, D., Hartmann, F., & Maas, V. S. (2008). Top management team heterogeneity, strategic change and operational performance. *British Journal of Management, 19*(3), 222–234.

Pettigrew, A. M. (1992). The character and significance of strategy process research. *Strategic Management Journal, 13*(S2), 5–16.

Rajagopalan, N., & Spreitzer, G. M. (1997). Toward a theory of strategic change: A multi-lens perspective and integrative framework. *Academy of Management Review, 22*(1), 48–79.

Romanelli, E., & Tushman, M. L. (1994). Organizational transformation as punctuated equilibrium: An empirical test. *Academy of Management Journal, 37*(5), 1141–1166.

Schilke, O., Hu, S., & Helfat, C. E. (2018). Quo Vadis, dynamic capabilities? A content-analytic review of the current state of knowledge and recommendations for future research. *Academy of Management Annals, 12*(1), 390–439.

Schwenk, C. R. (1988). The cognitive perspective on strategic decision making. *Journal of Management Studies, 25*(1), 41–55.

Seidman, D. (2021). *Why moral leadership matters now more than ever.* World Economic Forum.

Senge, P. M. (2006). *The fifth discipline: The art & practice of the learning organization.* Crown Publishing.

Shrivastava, P., & Grant, J. H. (1985). Empirically derived models of strategic decision-making processes. *Strategic Management Journal, 6*(2), 97–113.

Smith, K. G., & Grimm, C. M. (1987). Environmental variation, strategic change and firm performance: A study of railroad deregulation. *Strategic Management Journal, 8*(4), 363–376.

Solomon, R. C. (1992). *Ethics and excellence: Cooperation and integrity in business.* Oxford University Press.

Taylor, J. M., Santuzzi, A. M., & Cogburn, D. L. (2013). Trust and member satisfaction in a developing virtual organization: The roles of leader contact and experience with technology. *International Journal of Social and Organizational Dynamics in IT, 3*(1), 32–46.

Teece, D. J. (2007). Explicating dynamic capabilities: The nature and microfoundations of (sustainable) enterprise performance. *Strategic Management Journal, 28*(13), 1319–1350.

Teece, D. J., Pisano, G., & Shuen, A. (1997). Dynamic capabilities and strategic management. *Strategic Management Journal, 18*(7), 509–533.

Tuncdogan, A., Acar, O. A., & Stam, D. (2017). Individual differences as antecedents of leader behavior: Towards an understanding of multi-level outcomes. *The Leadership Quarterly, 28*(1), 40–64.

Tushman, M. L., & Romanelli, E. (1985). Organizational evolution: A metamorphosis model of convergence and reorientation. *Research in Organizational Behavior, 7*(2), 171–222.

Van de Ven, A. H., & Poole, M. S. (1995). Explaining development and change in organizations. *Academy of Management Review, 20*(3), 510–540.

Verburg, R. M., Bosch-Sijtsema, P., & Vartiainen, M. (2013). Getting it done: Critical success factors for project managers in virtual work settings. *International Journal of Project Management, 31*(1), 68–79.

Wagner, R. (2020). *What does leadership mean in an age of perpetual change?* World Economic Forum.

Westphal, J. D., & Fredrickson, J. W. (2001). Who directs strategic change? Director experience, the selection of new CEOs, and change in corporate strategy. *Strategic Management Journal, 22*(12), 1113–1137.

Whittington, R. (1996). Strategy as practice. *Long Range Planning, 29*(5), 731–735.

Whittington, R. (2001). The practice of strategy: Theoretical resources and empirical possibilities. *Proceedings of the EIASM Workshop on Micro Strategy and Strategising*, Brussels, Belgium, 1–3 February, 2001

Wood, J. (2022). *Hybrid working: Why there's a widening gap between leaders and employees.* World Economic Forum.

Zaccaro, S. J., Green, J. P., Dubrow, S., & Kolze, M. (2018). Leader individual differences, situational parameters, and leadership outcomes: A comprehensive review and integration. *The Leadership Quarterly, 29*(1), 2–43.

Zaccaro, S. J., Kemp, C., & Bader, P. (2004). Leader traits and attributes. *The Nature of Leadership, 101*, 124.

Zajac, E. J., & Kraatz, M. S. (1993). A diametric forces model of strategic change: Assessing the antecedents and consequences of restructuring in the higher education industry. *Strategic Management Journal, 14*(S1), 83–102.

Zajac, E. J., Kraatz, M. S., & Bresser, R. K. (2000). Modeling the dynamics of strategic fit: A normative approach to strategic change. *Strategic Management Journal, 21*(4), 429–453.

Zhang, Y., & Rajagopalan, N. (2010). Once an outsider, always an outsider? CEO origin, strategic change, and firm performance. *Strategic Management Journal, 31*(3), 334–346.

Zippia. (2022). 25 Trending Remote Work Statistics [2023]: Facts, Trends, And Projections. *Zippia.Com.* https://www.zippia.com/advice/remote-work-statistics/

5 Leadership and Decision-Making

Concluding Remarks

Federica Brunetta and Paolo Boccardelli

5.1 Leadership and Decision-Making: Concluding Remarks

Change and transformation have the capacity to not just "disrupt" industries, strategies, and operations but also to impact decision-making processes (e.g. Acciarini et al., 2020; Cristofaro, 2016; Reeves et al., 2021) and leadership paradigms (e.g. Caldwell et al., 2012; Lauer, 2021; Wagner, 2020). Managing change is a managerial challenge involving the combined efforts of individuals and groups within any organization (Canterino et al., 2020). Consequently, this book's aim has been to offer a review for both scholars and managers, particularly within the realms of decision-making and strategy, and to serve as a valuable resource and guide in navigating these transformative landscapes.

The collected insights and theories provide a comprehensive description of the inherent complexities that leading and decision-making face in times of change. Leadership and subsequent decision-making emerge as far from a solitary pursuit but rather as a dynamic interplay between individuals and their organizations, strategies, and environmental factors with (shared) vision, resilience, and capabilities being key elements at play.

Managing change is a multifaceted endeavor that encompasses both predictable and unforeseeable transformations – megatrends and disruptions, respectively (Cambridge University Press, 2024; European Commission, 2022). Decision-makers must play a pivotal role in identifying change and often have to rely on their capabilities to detect "weak signals" or "anomalies" (Ansoff, 1980; Reeves et al., 2021), predicting transformation and interpreting this change and its alignment with strategy.

Nonetheless, in line with extant research, we have discussed how cognitive biases may moderate decision-making processes (Das & Teng, 1999) and how institutional logics may also influence actors' cognition and provide different meanings and structures to their choices (Thornton & Ocasio, 2008) and the relationship to mission, strategy, identity, and core work (Besharov & Smith, 2014; Greenwood & Suddaby, 2006; Thornton et al., 2005). Of course, this delicate balance also requires finding the equilibrium between

DOI: 10.4324/9781003459804-5

intuition and rationality in decision-making process, which becomes crucial for decision-makers in turbulent times, necessitating both accuracy and speed in responding to emerging challenges (Akinci & Sadler-Smith, 2012; Allinson et al., 2000; Andersen, 2000; Cabantous & Gond, 2011; Calabretta et al., 2017; Clarke & Mackaness, 2001; Mouritsen, 1994; Simon, 1987).

After detecting change and planning accordingly, managers need to be able to implement new strategies and reorientate their organizations (Romanelli & Tushman, 1994; Tushman & Romanelli, 1985), so leadership capabilities are pivotal to navigating dynamic environments (e.g. Klemm, 2017). Leaders are required to be curious, resilient, collaborative, and flexible to manage today's uncertainty and volatility effectively. They are required to motivate and enable individuals to achieve goals, develop a collective vision, and lead transformation, following the idea of transformative leadership (Ciulla, 2005).

An emerging theme in the book has to do with digital transformation and the wider role of new technologies for leadership and decision-making, a topic that definitely will represent a rich avenue for future research. Recent disruptions and changes in business models quickly moved digitalization from an opportunity to an urgent need for most companies (Kraus et al., 2021), and managers can now leverage the potential of tools like big data and artificial intelligence (AI) to support decision-making processes. The impact of digital technologies on problem-solving, efficiency and effectiveness (Heavin & Power, 2018), and strategies (e.g. Bharadwaj et al., 2013; Intezari & Gressel, 2017; Kraus et al., 2021; Vial, 2019) is not new to literature. Nonetheless, there are major challenges and risks when it comes to understanding these technologies, possessing the competencies to harness their potential, and so adapting decision-making processes and leadership approaches (Vial, 2019).

Traditional paradigms for decision-making and the balance between rationality and intuition are being changed – and challenged – by technologies, specifically big data and AI (Gupta & George, 2016; Janssen et al., 2017; Merendino et al., 2018; Vidgen et al., 2017; Wang et al., 2016). In light of the availability of new and renewed knowledge bases, strategies can now significantly leverage organizational data through the use of extensive datasets, rapid analytical capabilities, and the integration of AI (Janssen et al., 2017). Managers must be able to develop capabilities (Merendino et al., 2018) related not only to interpreting and using such knowledge but also in terms of going deeper into technical aspects, such as critical inquiry, algorithm design, or the integration of diverse types of data, including structured (usually with precise format and meaning) and unstructured data (without a specific format and usually the result of unstructured interactions) in order to manage technical, strategical, and organizational dynamics associated with these technologies (Intezari & Gressel, 2017; Pauleen & Wang, 2017). Technologies may, then, enhance organizational knowledge, leading to additional value in decision-making beyond reducing time, optimizing operational processes, and simplifying information gathering, analysis, and interpretation (Gupta & George, 2016; Merendino et al., 2018; Pauleen & Wang, 2017).

Technological advancements have also changed leadership paradigms, with the challenges posed by remote leadership gaining prominence, accelerated by the initially sudden shift toward virtual work environments dictated by the COVID-19 disruption. Remote work is now regarded as an organizational means to increasing productivity, engagement, talent acquisition, and retention, thus, it is regarded as being highly critical for performance (Farrer, 2020). Leaders are often required to guide their teams remotely, even across different geographical areas and time zones, and they must do so by employing effective communication, fostering collaboration, and maintaining team cohesion despite distance, and therefore developing trust, emotional intelligence, self-awareness, and understanding (Dirks & Ferrin, 2002; Landry, 2019).

5.2 Conclusion

In essence, managing change isn't merely about reacting to dynamism in the environment; it's about proactively preparing for it. Foresight, strategic intuition, swift decision-making, technological awareness and capabilities, and leadership skills are crucial to success. Organizations aiming not just to be competitive but to master a competitive advantage must have a systemic and comprehensive approach, and managers need to act and prepare accordingly.

With this book, we aimed to provide a roadmap and discuss underlying elements related to navigating change, especially since decision-makers – and leaders – are continuously challenged with identifying and interpreting changes, whether that involves detecting the weak signals in trends or designing and implementing specific strategies. Of course, this also implies developing specific competencies to address, drive, and understand the trajectories of change, but also fostering organizational cultures oriented toward continuous learning and technological readiness. As the future unfolds and technology presents new challenges, a systemic and holistic approach remains indispensable for managers striving to succeed in an ever-changing world.

References

Acciarini, C., Brunetta, F., & Boccardelli, P. (2020). *Cognitive biases and decision-making strategies in times of change: A systematic literature review.* Management Decision.

Akinci, C., & Sadler-Smith, E. (2012). Intuition in management research: A historical review. *International Journal of Management Reviews, 14*(1), 104–122.

Allinson, C. W., Chell, E., & Hayes, J. (2000). Intuition and entrepreneurial behaviour. *European Journal of Work and Organizational Psychology*, *9*, 31–43.

Andersen, J. A. (2000). Intuition in managers: Are intuitive managers more effective?. *Journal of Managerial Psychology*, *15*, 46–63.

Ansoff, H. I. (1980). Strategic issue management. *Strategic Management Journal*, *1*(2), 131–148.

Besharov, M. L., & Smith, W. K. (2014). Multiple institutional logics in organizations: Explaining their varied nature and implications. *Academy of Management Review*, *39*, 364–381.

Bharadwaj, A., El Sawy, O. A., Pavlou, P. A., & Venkatraman, N. V. (2013). Digital business strategy: Toward a next generation of insights. *MIS Quarterly*, *37*(2), 471–482.

Cabantous, L., & Gond, J.-P. (2011). Rational decision making as performative praxis: Explaining Rationality's Éternel Retour. *Organization Science*, *22*, 573–586.

Calabretta, G., Gemser, G., & Wijnberg, N. M. (2017). The interplay between intuition and rationality in strategic decision making: A paradox perspective. *Organization Studies*, *38*, 225–261.

Caldwell, C., Dixon, R. D., Floyd, L. A., Chaudoin, J., Post, J., & Cheokas, G. (2012). Transformative leadership: Achieving unparalleled excellence. *Journal of Business Ethics*, *109*, 175–187.

Cambridge University Press. (2024). Disruption. In *Cambridge English Dictionary*. https://dictionary.cambridge.org/dictionary/english/disruption

Canterino, F., Cirella, S., Piccoli, B., & Shani, A. B. R. (2020). Leadership and change mobilization: The mediating role of distributed leadership. *Journal of Business Research*, *108*, 42–51.

Ciulla, J. B. (2005). *The quest for moral leaders*. Edward Elgar Publishing.

Clarke, I., & Mackaness, W. (2001). Management "intuition": An interpretative account of structure and content of decision schemas using cognitive maps. *Journal of Management Studies*, *38*, 147–172.

Cristofaro, M. (2016). Cognitive styles in dynamic decision making: A laboratory experiment. *International Journal of Management and Decision Making*, *15*(1), 53–82.

Das, T. K., & Teng, B. (1999). Cognitive biases and strategic decision processes: An integrative perspective. *Journal of Management Studies*, *36*(6), 757–778.

Dirks, K. T., & Ferrin, D. L. (2002). Trust in leadership: Meta-analytic findings and implications for research and practice. *Journal of Applied Psychology*, *87*(4), 611.

European Commission. (2022). *The Megatrends Hub. Competence Centre on Foresight*. https://knowledge4policy.ec.europa.eu/foresight/tool/megatrends-hub_en

Farrer, L. (2020). *5 Proven Benefits of Remote Work for Companies*. https://www.forbes.com/sites/laurelfarrer/2020/02/12/top-5-benefits-of-remote-work-for-companies/?sh=7dc7c0b416c8

Greenwood, R., & Suddaby, R. (2006). Institutional entrepreneurship in mature fields: The big five accounting firms. *Academy of Management Journal*, *49*(1), 27–48.

Gupta, M., & George, J. F. (2016). Toward the development of a big data analytics capability. *Information & Management*, *53*(8), 1049–1064.

Heavin, C., & Power, D. J. (2018). Challenges for digital transformation – towards a conceptual decision support guide for managers. *Journal of Decision Systems*, *27*(sup1), 38–45.

Intezari, A., & Gressel, S. (2017). Information and reformation in KM systems: Big data and strategic decision-making. *Journal of Knowledge Management*, *21*(1), 71–91.

Janssen, M., Voort, H., & Wahyudi, A. (2017). Factors influencing big data decision-making quality. *Journal of Business Research, 70,* 338–345.

Klemm, W. (2017). Leadership and creativity. Springer texts in business and economics. In Joan Marques, & Satinder Dhiman (Eds.) *Leadership Today* (chapter 15, pp. 263–278). Springer.

Kraus, S., Jones, P., Kailer, N., Weinmann, A., Chaparro-Banegas, N., & Roig-Tierno, N. (2021). Digital transformation: An overview of the current state of the art of research. *Sage Open, 11*(3), https://doi.org/10.1177/21582440211047576.

Landry, L. (2019). *Why emotional intelligence is important in leadership.* Harvard Business School.

Lauer, T. (2021). Change *management: Fundamentals and success factors* Springer.

Merendino, A., Dibb, S., Meadows, M., Quinn, L., Wilson, D., Simkin, L., & Canhoto, A. (2018). Big data, big decisions: The impact of big data on board level decision-making. *Journal of Business Research, 93,* 67–78.

Mouritsen, J. (1994). Rationality, institutions and decision making: Reflections on March and Olsen's rediscovering institutions. *Accounting, Organizations and Society, 19*(2), 193–211.

Pauleen, D. J., & Wang, W. Y. (2017). Does big data mean big knowledge? KM perspectives on big data and analytics. *Journal of Knowledge Management, 21*(1), 1–6.

Reeves, M., Goodson, B., & Whitaker, K. (2021). The power of anomaly: To achieve strategic advantage, scan the market for surprises. *Harvard Business Review.* July–Aug.

Romanelli, E., & Tushman, M. L. (1994). Organizational transformation as punctuated equilibrium: An empirical test. *Academy of Management Journal, 37*(5), 1141–1166.

Simon, H. A. (1987). Making management decisions: The role of intuition and emotion. *Academy of Management Executive, 1,* 57–64.

Thornton, P. H., Jones, C., & Kury, K. (2005). Institutional logics and institutional change in organizations: Transformation in accounting, architecture, and publishing. In C. Jones, and P. H. Thornton (Eds.) *Transformation in cultural industries* (Research in the sociology of organizations, Vol. 23, pp. 125–170), Emerald Group Publishing Limited, https://doi.org/10.1016/S0733-558X(05)23004-5

Thornton, P. H., & Ocasio, W. (2008). Institutional logics. In R. Greenwood, C. Oliver, R. Suddaby, & K. Sahlin-Andersson (Eds.), *The SAGE handbook of organizational institutionalism.* SAGE.

Tushman, M. L., & Romanelli, E. (1985). Organizational evolution: A metamorphosis model of convergence and reorientation. *Research in Organizational Behavior, 7*(2), 171–222.

Vial, G. (2019). Understanding digital transformation: A review and a research agenda. *The Journal of Strategic Information Systems, 28*(2), 118–144.

Vidgen, R., Shaw, S., & Grant, D. B. (2017). Management challenges in creating value from business analytics. *European Journal of Operational Research, 261*(2), 626–639.

Wagner, R. (2020). *What does leadership mean in an age of perpetual change?* World Economic Forum.

Wang, H., Xu, Z., Fujita, H., & Liu, S. (2016). Towards felicitous decision making: An overview on challenges and trends of big data. *Information Sciences, 367,* 747–765.

Index

For Product Safety Concerns and Information please contact our EU
representative GPSR@taylorandfrancis.com
Taylor & Francis Verlag GmbH, Kaufingerstraße 24, 80331 München, Germany

www.ingramcontent.com/pod-product-compliance
Ingram Content Group UK Ltd.
Pitfield, Milton Keynes, MK11 3LW, UK
UKHW021821240425
457818UK00006B/32

* 9 7 8 1 0 3 2 5 9 8 0 0 0 *